SCIENCE,
IDEOLOGY, AND
WORLD VIEW

SCIENCE, IDEOLOGY, AND WORLD VIEW

ESSAYS IN THE HISTORY OF EVOLUTIONARY IDEAS

John C. Greene

UNIVERSITY OF CALIFORNIA PRESS
Berkeley   Los Angeles   London

"Objectives and Methods in Intellectual History," *The Mississippi Valley Historical Review* 44 (1957): 58—74.

"The Kuhnian Paradigm and the Darwinian Revolution in Natural History," in *Perspectives in the History of Science and Technology*, Duane H. D. Roller, ed. University of Oklahoma Press, 1971. Pp. 3—25.

"Biology and Social Theory in the Nineteenth Century: Auguste Comte and Herbert Spencer," in *Critical Problems in the History of Science*, Marshall Clagett, ed. Madison: University of Wisconsin Press, 1959. Pp. 419—446.

"Darwin As a Social Evolutionist," *Journal of the History of Biology* 10 (1977): 1—27. Copyright © 1977 by D. Reidel Publishing Company, Dordrecht, Holland.

University of California Press
Berkeley and Los Angeles, California

University of California Press, Ltd.
London, England

Library of Congress Cataloging in
Publication Data

Greene, John C.
Science, ideology, and world view.

Includes index.
CONTENTS: Preface.—Science, ideology, and world view.—Objectives and methods in intellectual history.—[etc.]
1. Biology—Philosophy—History—Addresses, essays, lectures. 2. Evolution—History—Addresses, essays, lectures. 3. Science—Philosophy—History—Addresses, essays, lectures. I. Title.
QH331.G727   574.01   80-20756

Printed in the United States of America

1 2 3 4 5 6 7 8 9

For Crane Brinton

CONTENTS

PREFACE

The essays collected here were written over a period of twenty-three years. Taken together, they constitute a fairly unified interpretation of the interaction of science, ideology, and world view in the development of evolutionary biology in the last two centuries. They also serve as exemplars of the approach to the history of ideas set forth in the second essay. I have made very few changes in the previously published essays (nos. 2−5), largely because I am still satisfied with the ideas contained in them.

I am grateful to Professors Joel Kupperman, Harry Stout, Kentwood Wells, and Peter Rich, all of the University of Connecticut, for their suggestions with respect to one or more of the essays, and to my seminar students for their contributions to the discussion of Darwinian topics. I wish to express my appreciation to Peter Gautrey and Sidney Smith for assistance in deciphering Darwin's marginal notes, to the National Endowment for the Humanities for a Senior Fellowship that made these researches possible, and to the Master and Fellows of Corpus Christi College for extending the privileges of the college to me during my term as Senior Visiting Scholar. I am especially indebted to Professor Ernst Mayr of Harvard University for his vigorous criticisms of all of the essays. They forced me to clarify my own thinking and to take account of other points of view, even when I could not agree with them. I want also to thank Professor John Longhurst of the University of Kansas for helping to make this volume possible.

Finally, I acknowledge with gratitude the influence on my endeavors as an intellectual historian of Professor Crane

Brinton, whose course in European intellectual history and whose conversation at the Society of Fellows at Harvard University I recall with great pleasure. To him I have dedicated this collection of essays, some of which he was kind enough to speak well of.

John C. Greene

Storrs, Connecticut
April 1981

1

SCIENCE, IDEOLOGY, AND WORLD VIEW

The history of ideas has gone through some interesting transformations since the first essay in this collection was written during the heyday of "intellectual history" at mid-century. Social history has come into fashion, replete with concepts and tools borrowed from sociology, demography, anthropology, and psychology. Ideas have been assigned a secondary or tertiary role in historical development. Even the history of science, which had hitherto been focused on the genesis and filiation of ideas in the minds of scientific geniuses like Newton, Darwin, and Einstein, has felt the influence of the new historiography and broadened its focus to include the social, psychological, and cultural contexts in which science develops.

Without wishing to deny the utility of these new approaches to history or their relevance for the study of intellectual history, I think it is time to point out that they do not dispense with the need for a history of ideas, nor do they prove that ideas are less important in human history than population trends, economic developments, social mores, and psychological drives and complexes. The social historians themselves have been profoundly influenced not only by specific ideas of Karl Marx, Sigmund Freud, Max Weber, and other social theorists but also by the general idea of the possibility of a science of society, an idea derived ultimately from the successes of the physical sciences. The notion that ideas are epiphenomena reflecting changes in nonideational aspects of human society is itself an idea, and a self-defeating one at that. It propounds the paradox that the ultimate discovery of the human mind in its search for a rational

1

understanding of history is the discovery that ideas are unimportant in history. Carried to its logical conclusion, it consigns the hypotheses of the social historian himself to the realm of epiphenomena generated by the interplay of non-ideational factors in history. Taken seriously, it makes a mockery of science and of all intellectual effort.

How are we to escape this reduction to absurdity? Certainly not by pretending that science, philosophy, theology, and other forms of rational inquiry are totally insulated from the social, economic, psychological, and cultural contexts in which intellectual endeavor takes place. Even the sciences of nature can lay claim to no such intellectual purity. In the short run, science itself is shaped by existing knowledge and ideas. General conceptions of nature, God, knowledge, man, society, and history dictate what kind of science, if any, will be attempted, what methods will be employed, what topics will be investigated, what kinds of results will be expected; social norms define the value and purpose of these inquiries. In the long run, however, if the scientist has insight and intellectual integrity, his findings may alter the general conceptions that shaped his inquiry despite his own reluctance to give up received ideas. Or he may adopt a radical stance and use his findings as ideological weapons, extrapolating science into world view. Like some modern evolutionary biologists, he may find himself writing a book entitled *The Meaning of Evolution* or *Evolution in Action* or *Nature and Man's Fate*. The lines between science, ideology, and world view are seldom tightly drawn.

What we call science originated under very special circumstances in the eastern Mediterranean region, and its subsequent development was shaped by a multitude of influences: social, economic, and religious. But the one constant factor at work throughout this development was the intellectual drive toward a rational understanding of the world. Intellectual curiosity was not a sufficient cause for the rise of modern science, but it was a necessary and powerful one. This curiosity did not confine itself to what we call science. Philosophy and theology were the main forms taken by the search for rational understanding of reality before the seventeenth century. Newton's great treatise was entitled *Mathematical Principles of Natural Philosophy*, and the science of mechanics it set forth was intimately bound up with a mechanical philosophy of nature compounded of Greek atomism, Platonic mathematicism, and static Christian creationism. It continued to be so for two hundred years thereafter.

From the time of its birth, moreover, modern science had a powerful ideological component. Bacon and Descartes tried to assure church and state that they had nothing to fear from the "new philosophy," but Voltaire and Tom Paine argued otherwise, and Auguste Comte proclaimed the coming of a positivist order in which scientists, rather than priests, would be canonized. Inspired by the intellectual achievements of Newton, Euler, and Laplace, social theorists undertook to create a science of society, including a science of historical development. "Science" became a word to conjure with, and social theorists from Comte to Marx and Spencer claimed the Q.E.D. of science for their philosophies of history and society. Social Darwinism was laissez-faire political economy rendered "scientific" by association with Darwin's theory of natural selection. Meanwhile the progress of natural history and the earth sciences was undermining the static creationism that had permeated modern science since its inception.

It is this perpetual interplay of science, ideology, and world view that forms the subject matter of the essays in this volume. The first essay, addressed especially to American historians but also to historians of ideas generally, attempts to focus attention on changes in world view, defined as "the presuppositions of thought in given historical epochs." To illustrate the process by which dominant and subdominant world views take shape and undergo modification, it describes the static world view that prevailed at the birth of modern science and the gradual undermining of that view by the elaboration of the logical implications and speculative temptations implicit in the "mechanical philosophy," the seventeenth-century idea of nature as a divinely ordained, lawbound system of matter in motion. It gives due weight to the cumulative effect of the growth of empirical knowledge concerning the earth and its inhabitants and to the contributions of the scientists who made those discoveries, but it also shows those scientists subject to the pervasive influence of the static view of nature and sensitive in varying degrees to the ideological uses of the mechanical philosophy. It adumbrates the interplay between the natural sciences and social theory, a theme developed more fully in later essays. The essay closes with a discussion of the tension between science and religion in Western thought, a plea for "less emphasis on encyclopedic coverage and more on the search for basic patterns and for the factors that produce change in those patterns," and a suggestion that the kind of analysis recommended in the essay can profitably be applied to disclosing the presuppositions of thought in our own day. All this still seems sound to me. The ensuing essays, though not written with the maxims of "Objectives and Methods" in mind, illustrate some of the possibilities of the kind of historical investigation recommended there.

The second essay, written fourteen years after the first, takes the form of a critique of Thomas Kuhn's model for understanding changes in scientific thought. Since Kuhn drew his examples from the history of physical science, I thought it would be interesting to test his model with reference to the developments in natural history with which I became acquainted while working on my book *The Death of Adam: Evolution and Its Impact on Western Thought*. The essay is couched in Kuhnian terms, but the interpretations I suggest in opposition to his model are inspired by the conception of intellectual history set forth in my first essay. Kuhn's concept of a paradigm of scientific thought and practice is analogous in some ways to my idea of a pattern of thought, or dominant view of nature, but it applies only to scientists. Kuhn writes like a physicist turned historian of ideas. His paradigms are derived from the achievements of great scientists. They are undermined by discoveries made by scientists working within an existing paradigm. They are replaced by paradigms emerging from the intellectual endeavors of still other scientists. Kuhn concedes that scientific paradigms include epistemological and cosmological "commitments" transcending working scientific theories, but his scientists are not represented as being influenced by the general conceptions of nature, man, God, society, and history that inform the thought of their age, or as ideologically involved in social or political issues. His scientists confront nature and other scientists. Their community has its own history, sealed off from nonscientific influences though exerting a profound influence on ideas and events outside its domain.

In opposition to this view of things I have argued that scientists share the general preconceptions of their time; that these preconceptions change not simply because of new scientific discoveries, which are always subject to more than one interpretation, but more through the influence of alternative views of nature coexisting with the dominant view; that crises generated by the discovery of anomalous facts are not prerequisite to the elaboration of counterparadigms; that anomalous facts challenge world views as well as specific scientific theories and encounter opposition, even among scientists, for that reason; that the typical response to the challenge of anomalous facts is a compromise theory that minimizes the damage to traditional assumptions; that the challenge to a reigning paradigm may develop largely outside the relevant scientific community; that national intellectual and cultural traditions may predispose the scientists of a given nation to push their speculations in one direction rather than another; and, more particularly, that British political economy played a significant role in the emergence of theories of natural selection in the first half of the nineteenth century. These objections to the Kuhnian paradigm of paradigms still seem valid to me.

The third and fourth essays trace some interactions between biology and social theory, revealing a continual interplay of science, ideology, and world view. In Auguste Comte's writings, science becomes the means of reordering society on a new foundation, and the history and philosophy of science indicate the necessary stages by which this will be accomplished. Biology provides the clue to understanding human nature, and sociology, the science of historical development, discovers the "necessary chain of successive transformations" by which mankind, "starting from a condition barely superior to that of a society of great apes," has gradually ascended to its present high estate and will eventually be led onward to the establishment of a positive, or scientific, polity. In Herbert Spencer's writings there is the same confidence in science and its power to disclose the laws and stages of historical development, but social evolutionism is now linked to biological and cosmic evolutionism and harnessed in the service of the free-enterprise system. Social theory is "biologized" by means of an analogy between the competitive struggle in society and the "stern discipline of Nature" in the biological realm, and physics, biology, and sociology are united in an evolutionary world view combining the mechanical philosophy of the seventeenth century with the idea of progressive development in nature-history and the laissez-faire doctrines of British political economy. Science, ideology, and world view are interfused. British faith in progress through competitive struggle replaces French concern with the problem of social order.

The companion essay on Social Darwinism raises the question of Darwin's role in the development of a peculiarly British ideology of progress through relentless competition of individuals, tribes, nations, and races. Admirers of Darwin as a scientist and as a man have found it difficult to believe that he could have given credence to a social philosophy so repugnant to the mid-twentieth-century mind. For many of these persons, Darwin was the example par excellence of the hardheaded scientist who scorned to dabble in matters incapable of scientific verification or to extrapolate from biological to social theory. His known aversion to witnessing cruelty or suffering seemed incompatible with his acceptance of anything remotely resembling the Spencerian social philosophy. Accordingly, attempts to link Darwin with Malthus, Spencer, and the tradition of British political economy or with apologists for British imperialism were strenuously resisted. The purity of science, as well as Darwin's personal honor, seemed to be involved.

I do not pretend that the essay "Darwin as a Social Evolutionist" is the last word on this subject, but I hope that it will lay to rest the naive idea that Darwin was a "pure scientist" uncontaminated by the preconceptions of his age and culture. It is a curious fact that all, or nearly all, of the men who propounded some idea of natural selection in the first half of the nineteenth century were British. Given the international character of science, it seems strange that nature should divulge one of her profoundest secrets only to inhabitants of Great Britain. Yet she did. The fact seems explicable only by assuming that British political economy, based on the idea of the survival of the fittest in the marketplace, and the British competitive ethos generally predisposed Britons to think in terms of competitive struggle in theorizing about plants and animals as well as man. In any case, it should come as no surprise that Darwin's and Wallace's writings reflected the belief widespread among their countrymen in progressive improvement through individual, national, and racial competition.

The fifth essay, hitherto unpublished, fulfills the promise made at the end of the previous essay to "delineate a more general Spencerian-Darwinian world view on which Spencer, Darwin, Wallace, and Huxley converged about 1860, only to diverge again before the century had run its course." I do not flatter myself that this essay will establish a single usage for the word Darwinism—that would be expecting the impossible—but I hope it will provoke some discussion of the relationship between general scientific theories and the world views associated with them and of the problems of terminology raised by this relationship. The problem is especially acute in cases, like that of Darwin, in which the scientist eschews philosophy and ideology, leaving his readers to infer what they can about his general view of reality. Undoubtedly, some readers will conclude that such a scientist had no general view or views of this kind, but we have already seen how erroneous such a conclusion must be. The presuppositions of thought do not become less real when they are left unexpressed.

It may be objected, and doubtless will be, that Darwin, Spencer, Huxley, and Wallace had different intellectual temperaments, different intellectual histories, and different opinions on a wide variety of subjects. Wallace became a socialist and a believer in spiritualism, Huxley eventually rejected and excoriated Spencer's attempt to derive ethical guidance from the cosmic process, Spencer attacked Darwin for excessive reliance on natural selection, and Darwin criticized Spencer's unbounded confidence in the deliverances of speculative reason. But these differences should not be permitted to obscure the common outlook shared by these men in the early 1860s. That outlook deserves a name, and Darwinism is a convenient one, though Spencerianism-Darwinism may be more accurate historically. Once the existence of this world view has been acknowledged, attention can be directed to the tensions and ambivalences implicit in it, and the subsequent history of Darwinism can be spelled out in terms of the different ways in which each member of the quadrumvirate of English Darwinism responded to those ambiguities. Indeed, the problem of resolving those difficulties is still with us, as the final essay in this volume shows. Darwinism, in various transmuted forms, is alive and tolerably vigorous in our own time, as in the writings of leading evolutionary biologists like Julian Huxley, George Gaylord Simpson, Theodosius Dobzhansky, and Edward O. Wilson. To the historian of ideas these writings display the same interplay of science, ideology, and world view that characterized the works of Darwin and his contemporaries. They dispel, or at least should dispel, the dream of a purely scientific view of reality. Science is but a part, though an important one, of man's effort to understand himself, his culture, his universe.

2

OBJECTIVES AND METHODS IN INTELLECTUAL HISTORY

The rapid rise of intellectual history to prominence in the world of American scholarship has occasioned considerable comment in recent years. Most observers of this development have found it more remarkable for vitality and scope than for clarity as to aims, methods, and subject matter. In 1949 Merle Curti reported "much stirring and productivity" in the new domain of history but conceded that "basic methodological problems" remained largely unsolved.[1] In 1951 John Higham described American intellectual history as "still seeking coherence, still eluding confinement."[2] In a similar vein, Charles A. Barker attributed three main characteristics to the growing movement in both social and intellectual history: "its newness, its bigness, and its unorganized—that is to say its little-interpreted—condition."[3] More recently Henry L. Swint reported "an extreme looseness of definition and disparity of emphasis" in the courses offered in social and intellectual history in various institutions throughout the country. Although he disclaimed any intention to establish rigid boundary lines or to limit the free play of the mind, Swint nevertheless concluded that "Free discussion of terms, concepts, areas, and purposes should . . . result in a better understanding of the general purpose or goals of social history and of intellectual history and should to some extent clarify the confusion which apparently exists among specialists in the field."[4]

The consensus of these observers—specialists themselves—is that intellectual historians need to exchange ideas concerning aims and methods in their field of study. By way of contributing to such a discussion, the following pages offer a provisional definition of intellectual history, explain and illustrate the method of research implied in the definition, and argue the advantage to be gained by a wider application of this method in American intellectual history. No particular originality is claimed for the views presented. On the contrary, the author's debt to such writers as Alfred North Whitehead, Max Weber, Arthur O. Lovejoy, and Perry Miller should be obvious.[5] If the ensuing reflections contain anything new, it is the suggestion that the methods employed so successfully by these writers be applied more generally and more consistently in the study of American thought. It should be emphasized, however, that the author does not aim to construct a Procrustean bed in which everyone who would call himself an intellectual historian must lie. Every definition, every method, has its advantages and disadvantages. Doubtless the approach recommended here has its limitations, but in a field characterized by "extreme looseness of definition and disparity of emphasis" almost any definition is better than none. At the very least it may challenge others to formulate a more adequate one.[6]

In my view, the primary function of the intellectual historian is to delineate the presuppositions of thought in given historical epochs and to explain the changes that those presuppositions undergo from epoch to epoch. All history is intellectual history in some sense, but it is the peculiar province of the intellectual historian to search for and describe those most general ideas, or patterns of ideas, which inform the thought of an age, define its intellectual problems, and indicate the direction in which solutions are to be sought. The historian of science, for example, may study the origins of the doctrine of organic evolution, the student of political philosophy the development of natural-rights theory, the religious historian the debate concerning revealed and natural religion, but it is the intellectual historian whose special task it is to delineate the general conceptions of nature that informed men's thinking on all of these topics in a given era. Particular philosophies, ideologies, and scientific or artistic theories interest the student of the history of philosophy, politics, science, art, or literature. The more general patterns pervading the thought of an age are the object of the intellectual historian's attention. If he can delineate those patterns, he will have rendered a valuable service to all who study particular developments in the period, and it will be a service that he best can render.

But how does one discover the presuppositions of thought in a given age? The process involves both analysis and synthesis. This process might be illustrated in many ways, but it will be best to give one extended illustration from a period in which the author feels at home. Suppose then that one's aim is to delineate the dominant view of nature in the eighteenth century. One can dive in almost anywhere in either European or American sources—by examining the great debate between the friends of revelation and the advocates of natural religion, by reading the works of natural scientists, or by studying the poetry or political philosophy of the age. All that is needed is a wide coverage of material and a capacity to penetrate to implicit major premises. One soon discovers that these premises are related to each other and that an effort of synthesis is required to display their relations. It becomes apparent, moreover, that there was not just *one* pattern of thought in the epoch, but that there were several, some dominant, the others subdominant, incipient, or vestigial. These general modes of thought often coexisted in the mind of a single individual even when they were not entirely compatible with each other. They manifested themselves simultaneously in a single paragraph of his writings. They were not the particular views of particular individuals or even of particular groups of individuals; they were tendencies or patterns that the intellectual historian, aided by hindsight, discerns in the thought of the age.

To drive this point home it may be worthwhile to analyze in detail the underlying views of nature in the eighteenth century, defining that century broadly so as to include the period from Newton, whose *Principia* was first published in 1687, to Laplace, whose *Traité de Mécanique Céleste* was completed in 1825. After reading widely in writings on natural history and on natural and revealed religion in this period, the present writer arrived at the following formulation of the dominant view of nature.[7] Nature was conceived primarily as a framework of rationally contrived structures fitted as a stage for the activities of intelligent beings. The words *framework, structures,* and *stage* all express the dominant sentiment of the stability and permanence of the great features of nature: the fixed stars, the everlasting hills, the eternal seas, the created species. Change was recognized as a real aspect of nature, but a superficial aspect. It contributed variety to nature's panorama, but it could not alter her fundamental structures. Change might take the form of decline from original perfection, of cyclical movement serving to maintain the status quo, or of random variation about a norm, but in no case could it produce real novelty.

Closely linked to the idea of the permanence of the basic structures of nature was the conviction of their intelligent design. The framework of natural structures was regarded as divinely contrived to support the activities of intelligent, moral beings. Design and permanence went together, as did their antitheses, chance and change. The earth, since it was intended as a habitation for man, must have the stability and conformation requisite in a well-designed stage, however much accidental vicissitudes might alter the details. The same must be true of the planets and of all the other globes distributed throughout space. To the eighteenth-century mind, whether deist or Christian, it was axiomatic that matter existed to sustain mental and moral activity. The realms of space *must* be inhabited by intelligent beings, otherwise all those celestial bodies would have been created in vain. So it seemed to Sir William Herschel and to Tom Paine as well as to Archdeacon Paley and to the American clergyman and educator Timothy Dwight.

The perfect balance of nature was still another corollary of this general view of things. Whether in the motions of the solar system or in the mutual preying of animals on each other or in the cycle of geological processes on the surface of the earth, change in one direction was thought to be compensated by change in another, while nature as a whole remained unchanged. So fixed was this idea that when the evidence for the extinction of species and the disappearance of stars became too strong for disbelief, the breach in traditional attitudes was repaired by the calm assumption that nature had made provision for replacing these losses.

This is not to say that all of the elements of this pattern of thought were peculiar to the eighteenth century. On the contrary, many of them can be traced back to the Greeks, and not a few have survived to the present day. It was the combination, or general pattern, of ideas that was peculiar to the Newtonian period broadly defined. It would be possible to describe this pattern more fully and to illustrate its ubiquity by examples drawn from various fields of thought. One thinks, for example, of the notion of linguistic decay, of the myth of the social contract, of Blumenbach's theory of race formation by degeneration from the original model of the human species, of Linnaeus's contempt for varieties as the "sports of nature," of Paine's conception of the solar system as a schoolroom designed by the Almighty Lecturer, of Jefferson's bland assurance that God would not place man on earth without giving him a moral sense, of Newton's argument for the divine origin of the solar system, and of many other manifestations of the same habit of thought. The main argument will be better served, however, by considering the relations of this dominant view of nature to a subdominant, or incipient, view of nature that took root in the seventeenth century, developed in uneasy subordination to the dominant view for nearly two centuries, and eventually emerged dominant itself, though in a somewhat modified form, in the late nineteenth century. This was the conception of nature as a law-bound system of matter in motion, the cosmology elaborated in the seventeenth century by the founders of the science of mechanics—Galileo, Descartes, Huyghens, and Newton—and neatly summarized in Newton's speculation that "God in the Beginning form'd Matter in solid, massy, hard, impenetrable, moveable Particles, of such Sizes and Figures, and with such other Properties, and such Proportion to Space, as most conduced to the end for which he form'd them."[8]

The bearing of this cosmology on the doctrine of special providence is well understood; not so its bearing on the view of nature just described. In some respects the mechanical cosmology bore the imprint of the dominant view of nature. Newton's impenetrable atom was an example par excellence of a permanent structure that participated in the world of change without being altered thereby. The atom simply was what it was because God had designed it a certain way and intended it to stay that way. But however immutable the atom might be, the idea that visible nature is produced by the combinations and permutations of a system of material particles in motion had disturbing implications for the dominant view of nature, the view expressed in John Ray's definition of the works of the creation as "the Works created by God at first, and by him conserved to this Day in the same State and Condition in which they were first made."⁹ There was nothing in the idea of a law-bound system of matter in motion to suggest the stability of the structures produced by its functioning. Mutability, not stability, was the logical outcome of such a system, and, since every state of the system proceeded by rule from the preceding state, it was hard to see why any state should be regarded as initial or as final. As Kant was to show in the following century, the argument from design could be saved only by supposing that the Creator had planned the history of nature *ab initio*.¹⁰ But these implications of the new science and cosmology were slow to develop. Newton and Boyle were aware of them, but they managed to reconcile the conception of nature as a system of matter in motion with the dominant view of the stability and wise design of the fundamental structures of nature by supposing that God had so contrived the properties of matter and the laws of motion that they would perpetually produce the stable world required for His moral purpose.¹¹ A long road stretched from Robert Boyle's *Origin of Forms and Qualities*, published in 1666, to Charles Darwin's *Origin of Species*, and on every mile of that road the progress toward an evolutionary view of nature was impeded by the deeply ingrained conviction that nature was a framework of rationally contrived structures adapted to support the activities of intelligent beings. The dominant view did not yield its supremacy without a severe and protracted struggle.

Almost imperceptibly the discussion has shifted from the problem of delineating the presuppositions of thought in a given period to the problem of explaining how and why a dominant view ceases to be dominant and a subdominant view achieves dominance. This is as it should be, for only by describing the patterns of thought at two different moments in history can the historian mark out a movement of thought. Before one can explain an intellectual development, one must be able to define it by indicating the *terminus a quo* and the *terminus ad quem*. This task of definition requires of the historian a broad exposure to the relevant source materials, a logical habit of mind, and a keen eye for the recurrence of the telltale words and phrases that unlock the thought habits of a bygone age. When an eighteenth-century writer uses the adjectives *fixed, appointed, assigned,* or conversely, *accidental* or *adventitious,* that is when he unconsciously shows his hand. It makes little difference for this purpose whether he is a "great thinker" or just a country parson grinding out a sermon. Noah Webster's *History of Animals* or Jefferson's *Notes on the State of Virginia* will do quite as well as Linnaeus's *System of Nature* or Kant's *Natural History and Theory of the Heavens.* The greater the range and variety of source materials, the more certain one is that the pattern that emerges is indeed a general pattern, the pattern of the age.

But when, after defining a movement of thought, one seeks to explain how and why it took place, the problem becomes infinitely more complicated. It is no longer a simple matter of textual analysis, for a great many nonlogical factors play a part in transitions of thought. True, there is an internal development of thought arising out of the intellectual effort of successive generations of thinkers. In this development the great thinker plays a peculiarly important part, the analysis of which will always be one of the major tasks of the intellectual historian. But the intellectual discoveries and mythopoeic creations of men of genius are only single strands in the complicated web of causes that produces a movement of thought. World view exerts an enormous influence, ideology speeds or delays the transitions of thought in behalf of partisan purpose, and technology alters drastically the conditions of life, thereby changing human receptivity to certain ideas and attitudes. To ascertain the exact force of these and other causal influences in producing a major change of intellectual habit seems impossible, but the intellectual historian must make as close an approximation as he can.

Here again an example is in order. If one attempts to explain the great movement of thought that led from John Ray's *The Wisdom of God Manifested in the Works of the Creation*, published in 1691, to Herbert Spencer's *First Principles*, and from Boyle's *Origin of Forms and Qualities* to Darwin's *Origin of Species*, one must take into consideration a great many causal factors. One must consider, for example, the cumulative effect of the growth of empirical knowledge concerning the earth and its inhabitants, the discoveries resulting from technical innovations, and the contribution of scientific genius, whether, as in the case of Linnaeus and Cuvier, the contribution was made within the context of received ideas concerning nature, or whether, as in the case of Buffon, Erasmus Darwin, and Lamarck, it consisted in a restless search for a new key to old problems, involving a determined attempt to throw off the omnipresent influence of the dominant view of nature by exploring the implications of the subdominant view. One must also consider the extent to which ideological conflict drew out the implications of the new science and cosmology. The reformers of the eighteenth century found in the Newtonian system of matter in motion a convenient symbol of the kind of society they hoped to usher in—a society in which the activities of innumerable individuals, each pursuing his own happiness, would eventuate by divine contrivance in the general welfare of mankind. In Newton's demonstration of the motions of the solar system these reformers found a perfect physical model of their social ideal, a model that seemed to vindicate that ideal by proving it "natural." At the same time the conception of nature as a law-bound system of matter in motion could be used to discredit the Scriptural sanctions invoked by conservatives in defense of antiquated institutions, for did it not exclude the possibility of miracles, including those miracles that were supposed to prove the divine origin of the Bible and of the

Christian dispensation? Clearly, the world-machine had its polemical uses in the struggle for reform in the eighteenth century. In the next century the Marxians would push its logic even further in an attempt to discredit not only Christianity but liberal bourgeois society as well. Materialism and mutability would be extended to the realm of social thought. It was Marx, it will be recalled, who declared that "the present society is no solid crystal, but an organism capable of change and . . . constantly changing."[12]

The drawing out of the implications of the seventeenth-century cosmology undermined many traditional conceptions—the doctrine of the plenary inspiration of Scripture, the conviction of the stability of nature, the notion that matter is subordinate to mind, the cosmological argument from design—but it could not in itself suggest the idea of evolution, or progressive improvement, in nature. The advance of this idea in biology resulted from a variety of causes, too numerous and complex to discuss fully here. The gradual uncovering of the fossil record was one factor, but an earlier and more pervasive influence on biological thought was the general sense of progressive improvement in society; and this in turn had economic and technological, as well as intellectual roots. The extension to the cosmic order of the growing social and historical optimism is illustrated in Erasmus Darwin's suggestion "that all nature exists in a state of perpetual improvement by laws impressed on the atoms of matter by the great CAUSE OF CAUSES." "This idea," he declared, "is analogous to the improving excellence observable in every part of the creation; such as in the progressive increase of the wisdom and happiness of its inhabitants; and is consonant to the idea of our present situation being a state of probation, which by our exertions we may improve."[13]

Many other factors in the transition to an evolutionary conception of nature deserve attention, but those already mentioned should suffice to indicate the types of investigation involved in a causal analysis of a major intellectual movement. It should be recognized, however, that abstract analysis is not the final goal of the intellectual historian's labors. The end product of research in intellectual history, as in all history, should be a narrative that not only tells what happened and how and why it happened but makes it happen again for the reader. To accomplish this task the intellectual historian must pay attention to the affective tone of general ideas and to their concrete manifestations in language, literature, art, and popular myth. He must realize, for example, that every world view involves an emotional, as well as an intellectual, apprehension of nature. When nature is conceived as an artifact contrived by a transcendent God, the contemplation of nature evokes delight and wonder at the divine ingenuity. But when God is thought to be immediately present in nature, admiration gives way to rapture: "God, I can push the grass apart, And lay my finger on thy heart." Thus, sensitivity to affective tone is as requisite in the study of intellectual history as analytical acumen. Without it the historian can never reach beyond description and causal analysis to re-create the past and make it live again in men's imaginations.

So much concerning intellectual history in general. What of American intellectual history in particular? At first blush it may seem that investigations of the kind described have little to do with American intellectual history. They belong, it may be urged, to the general history of Western thought and concern developments in Europe more than those in America. They may provide useful background material for studies in American intellectual history, but they are not of its essence, hence they should be left to students of European thought. America for the Americans; Europe for the Europeans.

This Monroe Doctrine in intellectual history is entirely untenable. The peculiarity of general ideas is their ubiquity in time and place. Western thought is all of a piece. It cannot be chopped up into centuries and countries without rendering it lifeless and meaningless. American thought is but an aspect of Western thought, inseparable from it in any effective sense. The truth of this proposition should be apparent from what has already been said about views of nature in the eighteenth century. By way of more concrete illustration, however, it may be worthwhile to consider a specific development in American thought, such as, for example, the conflict between science and religion. Now the conflict between science and religion has undoubtedly had some special features in America that were not present in the same degree in a predominantly Catholic country, such as France, or in a Protestant country with an established church, such as England, nor is there any question that these and other national peculiarities require special study. But surely one should try to understand the general nature of the conflict between science and religion before undertaking to study its distinctive manifestations in the American environment. How is one to know what is peculiar and unique until one knows what is common and general? Here is a pitfall into which many have stumbled by trusting to secondary accounts or to a brief survey of European writers to form their ideas of the general state of knowledge and opinion. Some historians, for example, have thought to find distinctively American causes for ideas and attitudes in Jeffersonian America without realizing that these thought patterns were common in the Western world long before Jefferson's time.

But to return to the conflict between science and religion, how can the general nature of this conflict be understood without a searching inquiry into the structure of Western thought? Consider, for example, the overwhelming importance in this conflict of the doctrine of the plenary inspiration of Scripture, the doctrine that maintains that the Bible is of divine origin and that everything in it, properly understood, is substantially true.[14] The influence of this doctrine in American thought has been insufficiently appreciated. One looks in vain in most books on American intellectual history for a satisfactory exposition of the doctrine. One reads, of course, that the Bible was very important in American thought, that it was regarded as divinely inspired, that the progress of natural science and Biblical criticism did much to impair belief in Scripture, but except in a very few books, one fails to learn in what sense it was believed to be inspired, what rules were laid down for its interpretation, what were the "internal" and "external" evidences supporting the belief in its divine origin, what arguments were advanced to show the inherent probability that God would make such a revelation to man, or what grounds were alleged for expecting such a revelation to be mysterious to human reason. Still less does one form any conception of the influence of the doctrine or of the intellectual and spiritual consequences of its decline.

To illustrate: the assumption of plenary inspiration by the friends of revelation dictated their way of conceiving the conflict between science and religion. What was science from their point of view? It was the study of God's truth as revealed in His works. What was theology? It was the study of God's truth as revealed in His Word. But surely God's truth could not conflict with God's truth, hence there could be no real conflict between science and religion. Any apparent conflict must result either from faulty science or from a faulty interpretation of Scripture. So the argument ran, and it is impossible to understand the wearisome series of reconciliations of science and the Bible by eminent scientists like Benjamin Silliman, James Dwight Dana, and Edward Hitchcock without first grasping their reasons for believing that science and Scripture must agree.[15]

The decline of belief in the plenary inspiration of Scripture had important intellectual and spiritual consequences. The point to be stressed is that the Bible so conceived provided a key to the great problem of man's origin, duty, and destiny, a problem to which most men feel the need of some answer. Believers in plenary inspiration might disagree as to the interpretation of Scripture, but they were united in the conviction that the Bible properly interpreted could teach man categorically and infallibly what it most concerned him to know. The decay of belief in plenary inspiration thus precipitated a search for a new key to the problem of human destiny. The deists thought to find it in nature and reason, but what their reason found in nature was little more than what Christian natural theology had taught them to expect to find there. The transcendentalists were the pietists of natural religion. They, too, looked to nature for the key to man's situation in the universe, but not to nature conceived as a system of matter in motion. For them, nature was the immediate manifestation of the divine presence, the garment of the living God. As the implications of the mechanical cosmology for the dominant view of nature were progressively revealed, both deists and transcendentalists were thrown on the defensive. Some men turned to history to find a clue to the meaning of human life; others to psychology; others made a religion of science. Whatever the direction, the quest was the same. It was a search for a key such as that which had once been provided by a book believed to be divinely inspired and infallibly correct in everything it said.

If we probe still deeper into the conflict between science and religion, the hopelessness of attempting to study it in a purely American context becomes even more apparent. Not only the doctrine of plenary inspiration but also the dominant view of nature was crumbling before the onslaught of science. This process, already under way in the eighteenth century, developed rapidly in the nineteenth, affecting Christians, deists, and transcendentalists alike. Unfortunately, most writers have paid little attention to this development in the pre-Darwinian era. As a result, the treatment of Darwinism itself has been inadequate.

On its profoundest level, the conflict between science and religion involves an issue concerning the possibility of knowledge and the reliability of various ways of knowing. It is on this level that the conflict is taking place today. Surely our intellectual histories should acquaint the student with the general outlines of this great issue. They should cut beneath the bare exposition of pragmatism, instrumentalism, and other isms to the underlying tensions in Western thought, tensions that have manifested themselves in a thousand forms and contexts from the time of Plato and Aristotle to the present day. In short, the American intellectual historian must be first and foremost an intellectual historian and only secondarily an American historian.

Certain advantages may be expected to follow from a wider application of this approach to intellectual history. First, it gives to the intellectual historian a definite field of his own, with a clearly defined subject matter related in an intelligible way to the subject matter of surrounding disciplines. Although the intellectual historian works with the same materials that are used by the political historian, the student of literature, and the historian of science, he handles them in a different way with a different object in view. His findings, far from competing with those of scholars in related disciplines, should prove very useful to them. How thankful would the student of Progressivism be for a clear delineation of the most general presuppositions of thought regarding nature, human nature, and society in the world of the late nineteenth century! He himself may contribute to such a delineation, of course, but that is not his main concern. He must look to the intellectual historian for a general orientation in Western thought.

The second advantage follows from the first. It consists in helping to place American ideas in proper perspective and thus to set off their uniqueness and originality where they have any. It guards against naïve attempts to explain intellectual developments solely in terms of the frontier or some other peculiarly American influence. It places a damper on chauvinism and discourages parochialism.

Third, it makes for a more balanced approach to American intellectual history. Anyone concerned with discovering the presuppositions of American thought and explaining their transformations will find it difficult to neglect religious thought as, in general, it has been neglected except for certain phases that have excited interest because of their bearing on literature, politics, or reform. The failure of American intellectual historians to reckon adequately with the doctrine of the plenary inspiration of Scripture is relevant in this connection. It is noteworthy, also, that the vast majority of Americans in the mid-nineteenth century belonged to churches that described themselves as evangelical; yet, although we have many studies of transcendentalism, we have no general intellectual portrait of evangelical orthodoxy. It is natural, of course, that the directions of research in intellectual history should be dictated to a considerable extent by the personal interests of the researcher, but these cannot be his sole guide. Account must also be taken of the interests of the people whom he is investigating. If he is looking for the presuppositions of thought in seventeenth-, eighteenth-, or nineteenth-century America, he cannot avoid prolonged study of religious writings, theology included.

Fourth, the search for basic presuppositions demands and encourages an analytical habit of mind, which is much needed in American intellectual history. There are several comprehensive descriptive accounts of American thought, but of works that attempt to analyze the structure of thought in given periods and to account in a systematic fashion for fundamental shifts of intellectual outlook there have been all too few. Notable exceptions, such as Perry Miller's studies of Puritanism, come to mind, but the fact remains that most writers on American intellectual history have been content to describe the surface of American thought. These accounts are highly useful, but they need to be supplemented and illuminated by studies that penetrate to fundamental presuppositions, delineate the dominant and subdominant patterns of thought, and thus prepare the way for attempts at causal explanation. Thus, for example, simple descriptive accounts of mesmerism, spiritualism, adventism, hydropathy, and similar mid-nineteenth-century phenomena are much to be desired, but studies of this kind in no way obviate the necessity for an approach that treats these phenomena collectively and undertakes, by a close analysis of the writings associated with them, to discover their lowest common denominator and thus to reveal some basic relations between new and old patterns of thought. This kind of undertaking requires careful training in textual analysis, training aimed at developing an analytical habit of mind. The practice required is in close examination of source materials for the underlying premises, with special attention to the connotations of words and to the recurrence of stock phrases and of situations in which the writer seems to be trying to adhere simultaneously to mutually incompatible patterns of thought. Training of this sort is extremely valuable for the teaching and writing of all forms of history. In intellectual history it is indispensable. Some historians suppose that simple descriptive studies can provide building blocks for reconstructing the general patterns of thought in a given period, but this is not the case.

Such studies may yield a general impression of their subject and some occasional insights, but unless the author has attempted to discover underlying presuppositions, the reader is left with nothing but vague hunches and speculations to the effect, for example, that mesmerism, hydropathy, and similar phenomena may have been related to the frontier experience, to the mobility of American life, or to the insecurity of such and such a class. Hunches of this kind are valuable, but their verification requires systematic studies of the kind indicated.

Finally, the adoption of a more analytical approach to intellectual history should enable the intellectual historian to participate more effectively in cross-disciplinary projects. Historians have been urged to adapt the methods and tools of the social sciences to the study of history, but seldom have they seemed to realize that they have a contribution to make in return, especially in the field of intellectual history. For why should not the type of analysis that enables the intellectual historian to reconstruct the thought patterns of past ages prove equally serviceable in discovering the tensions in modern thought? It is true, of course, that the presuppositions of thought in the present age are those of the intellectual historian himself, and that he will therefore have difficulty in recognizing them for what they are. Nevertheless, it should be possible for an intellectual historian steeped in the thought of earlier periods and rendered sensitive by long practice to the underlying assumptions of written discourse to assist modern scientists, social scientists, historians, and others by calling attention to the thought patterns implicit in their writings. This may seem more a task for a logician than for an intellectual historian, but the time dimension is all-important. The tendencies and habits of thought that are dredged up by analysis have a long history, and the understanding of that history is relevant to the clarification of thought in the present. No other person is so well equipped for this task as the intellectual historian, for he specializes in describing patterns of thought and explaining their transformations.

The possibilities for intellectual collaboration of this kind are enormous. Social scientists in particular would benefit greatly from a systematic analysis of their writings by well-trained intellectual historians, nor is there any doubt that the historians themselves would learn something in the process. But intellectual history must have its own discipline before it can contribute much to cross-disciplinary studies. It must place less emphasis on encyclopedic coverage and more on the search for basic patterns and for the factors that produce change in those patterns. What it sacrifices in scope it will gain in clarity and force. These considerations apply to all intellectual history but especially to American intellectual history, which, as Professor Higham puts it, is "still seeking coherence, still eluding confinement."

In conclusion, it should be reemphasized that no single approach to the study of the history of ideas is sufficient in itself. Tastes vary, problems vary, and every individual makes his contribution in his own way. To the present author it seems that a wider application of the approach here recommended would have beneficial effects on the study and writing of American intellectual history. But mere prescriptions and recipes do not constitute intellectual history. The proof of the pudding is in the eating, the proof of intellectual history in the reading.

NOTES

1. Quoted in Thomas C. Cochran, "A Decade of American Histories," *Pennsylvania Magazine of History and Biography* 73 (1949): 153.

2. John Higham, "The Rise of American Intellectual History," *American Historical Review* 46 (1951): 453.

3. Charles A. Barker, "Needs and Opportunities in American Social and Intellectual History," *Pacific Historical Review* 20 (1951): 3, 7.

4. Henry L. Swint, "Trends in the Teaching of Social and Intellectual History," *Social Studies* 46 (1955): 243, 249.

5. Grateful acknowledgment is also made to the following persons for stimulating and helpful criticism of this essay: Merle Curti, Crane Brinton, Richard H. Shryock, Bert J. Loewenberg, Henry F. May, Charles A. Barker, George L. Mosse, Roy H. Pearce,

Stow Persons, Arthur Bestor, Robert A. Lively, Charles G. Sellers, John W. Ward, Thomas LeDuc, Arthur M. Schlesinger, Sr.

6. For other recent attempts to define intellectual history and its problems see, for example, Crane Brinton, *Ideas and Men: The Story of Western Thought* (New York, 1950), introduction; Franklin L. Baumer, "Intellectual History and Its Problems," *Journal of Modern History* 21 (1949): 191–203; John Higham, "Intellectual History and Its Neighbors," *Journal of the History of Ideas* 15 (1954): 339–47.

7. The following titles selected from various fields of thought afford a sample of the kinds of source materials from an examination of which the present delineation of views of nature in the eighteenth century was constructed: John Ray, *The Wisdom of God Manifested in the Works of the Creation*, 3rd ed. (London, 1701); William Paley, *Natural Theology: or, Evidences of the Existence and Attributes of the Deity, Collected from the Appearances of Nature*, 3rd ed. (London, 1803); William Smellie, *The Philosophy of Natural History* (Dover, N.H., 1808); Timothy Dwight, *Theology Explained and Defended, in a Series of Sermons*, 12th ed., 4 vols. (New York, 1846); William M. Van der Weyde, ed., *The Life and Works of Thomas Paine*, 10 vols. (New York, 1925); Ethan Allen, *Reason the Only Oracle of Man: or a Compendious System of Natural Religion* (New York and Philadelphia, 1836); Carolus Linnaeus, *A General System of Nature*, trans. William Turton, 7 vols. (London, 1806); Georges Cuvier, *The Animal Kingdom Arranged in Conformity with its Organization*, trans. M. M'Murtrie, 4 vols. (New York, 1831); Pierre Simon Laplace, *The System of the World, trans.* Henry H. Harte, 2 vols. (Dublin, 1830); Immanuel Kant, *Kant's Cosmogony as in His Essay on the Retardation of the Rotation of the Earth and His Natural History and Theory of the Heavens*, ed. and trans. William Hastie (Glasgow, 1900); Saul K. Padover, ed., *The Complete Jefferson* (New York, 1943); Jedidiah Morse, *The American Geography*, 2nd ed. (London, 1792); Samuel Stanhope Smith, *An Essay on the Causes of the Variety of Complexion and Figure in the Human Species*, 2nd ed. (New Brunswick, 1810); Peter Shaw, ed., *The Philosophical Works of the Honourable Robert Boyle, Esq.*, 2nd ed., 3 vols. (London, 1738); Georges Louis Le Clerc (Comte de Buffon), *Natural History, General and Particular*, trans. William Smellie, 2nd ed., 9 vols. (London, 1785); Jared Sparks, ed., *The Works of Benjamin Franklin*, 10 vols. (Chicago, 1882), VI. Specific illustrations of the dominant view of nature may be found in the present writer's "Some Early Speculations on the Origin of Human Races," *American Anthropologist* 56 (1954): 31–41, and "Some Aspects of American Astronomy 1750–1815," *Isis* 45 (1954): 339–58.

8. Isaac Newton, *Opticks: or, A Treatise of the Reflections, Refractions, Inflections, and Colours of Light*, 4th ed. (London, 1730): 375–76. See also Robert Boyle, *The Origin of Forms and Qualities; Serving as an Introduction to the Mechanical Philosophy*, in Shaw, ed., *Philosophical Works of Robert Boyle*, 1:214–15.

9. Ray, *Wisdom of God*, preface.

10. "Matter, which is the primitive constituent of all things, is . . . bound to certain laws, and when it is freely abandoned to these laws it must necessarily bring forth beautiful combinations. It has no freedom to deviate from this perfect plan. Since it is thus subject to a supremely wise purpose, it must necessarily have been put into such harmonious relationships by a First Cause ruling over it; and there is a God, just because nature even in chaos cannot proceed otherwise than regularly and according to order." Immanuel Kant, *Universal Natural History and Theory of the Heavens*, in Hastie, *Kant's Cosmogony*, p. 23.

11. See Newton, *Opticks*, pp. 377–78, for evidence of his uneasiness about the temptation to derive the structures of nature, including the solar system, from the combinations and permutations of the system of matter in motion: "For it became who created them [the ultimate particles of matter] to set them in order. And if he did so, it's unphilosophical to seek for any other Origin of the World, or to pretend that it might arise out of a Chaos by the mere Laws of Nature." See also Boyle, *Excellence and Grounds of the Mechanical Philosophy*, in Shaw, *Philosophical Works*, 1: 187: "nor do I suppose, when God had put into the whole mass of matter, an invariable quantity of motion, he needed do no more to make the universe; the material parts being able, by their own unguided motions, to throw themselves into a regular system."

12. Karl Marx, *Capital: A Critical Analysis of Capitalist Production*, trans. from 3rd German ed. Samuel Moore and Edward Aveling (New York, 1890), "Preface to the First Edition," p. 16.

13. Erasmus Darwin, *Zoonomia: or, the Laws of Organic Life*, 4th Amer. ed., 2 vols. (Philadelphia, 1818) 1: 400–401, 437.

14. "The true definition of inspiration, then, is SUCH A DIVINE INFLUENCE UPON THE MINDS OF THE SACRED WRITERS AS RENDERED THEM EXEMPT FROM ERROR, BOTH IN REGARD TO THE IDEAS AND THE WORDS. This is properly called PLENARY inspiration. Nothing can be conceived more satisfactory. Certainty, infallible certainty, is the utmost that can be desired in any *narrative*; and if we have this in the sacred Scriptures, there is nothing more to be wished in regard to

this matter." Archibald Alexander, *Evidences of the Authenticity, Inspiration, and Canonical Authority of the Holy Scriptures* (Philadelphia: Presbyterian Board of Publication, n.d.), p. 230. Alexander was a professor of theology at the Presbyterian Seminary in Princeton in the mid-nineteenth century. For a Congregationalist view of plenary inspiration see Timothy Dwight, "On Revelation," *Sermons*, 2 vols. (New Haven, 1828) 2: 61–78. The classic work on the evidences of Christianity, used for many years in American colleges, was William Paley's *A View of the Evidences of Christianity*, first published in London in 1794. It should be emphasized that the discussion in the present article refers only to the belief in the *plenary* inspiration of Scripture. Unitarians, such as Joseph Priestley and William Ellery Channing, believed in the inspiration of Scripture, but not in plenary inspiration. See William E. Channing, *A Discourse on the Evidences of Revealed Religion, Delivered before the University in Cambridge, at the Dudleian Lecture, March 14, 1821* (Boston, 1821).

15. Thus, the oceanographer Matthew F. Maury laid it down as a rule of conduct "never to forget who is the Author of the great volume which nature spreads out before us, & always to remember that the same Being is also the Author of the book which Revelation holds up to us; & though the two works are entirely different, their records are equally true; & when they bear upon the same point . . . it is as impossible that they should contradict each other as it is that either should contradict itself. If the two cannot be reconciled, the fault is ours, & it is because, in our blindness & weakness, we have not been able to interpret aright, either the one or the other or both." Maury to "My dear Sir," Washington, D. C., 22 January 1855, Maury Collection, Division of Manuscripts, Library of Congress, Washington, D. C. It is interesting to observe how many of the ablest American scientists of Maury's day were evangelical in their faith and believers in the plenary inspiration of the Bible. The view of nature implicit in such a faith seems to have been more conducive to the study of natural science that that which informed transcendentalism.

SUGGESTED FURTHER READING

Crane Brinton, "Intellectual History," in David L. Sills, ed., *International Encyclopedia of Social Sciences* (New York: Macmillan, 1968) 6: 462–468.

Hajo Holborn, "The History of Ideas," *American Historical Review*, 72 (1968): 683–695.

Hayden V. White, "The Tasks of Intellectual History," *The Monist* 53 (1969): 606–630.

Paul K. Conkin, "Intellectual History: Past, Present and Future," in Charles F. Delzell, ed., *The Future of History: Essays in the Vanderbilt University Centennial Symposium* (Nashville: Vanderbilt University Press, 1977), pp. 111–133.

Robert Allen Skotheim, *American Intellectual Histories and Historians* (Princeton: Princeton University Press, 1966).

John Higham and Paul K. Conkin, eds., *New Directions in American Intellectual History* (Baltimore and London: The Johns Hopkins University Press, 1979).

3

THE KUHNIAN PARADIGM AND THE DARWINIAN REVOLUTION IN NATURAL HISTORY

The publication of Thomas Kuhn's *The Structure of Scientific Revolutions* in 1962 was an important milestone in the development of the historiography of science. It was the first attempt to construct a generalized picture of the process by which a science is born and undergoes change and development. The main stages of development envisaged by Kuhn's model may be summarized as follows:

1. A preparadigm stage in which the natural phenomena that later form the subject matter of a mature science are studied and explained from widely differing points of view.
2. The emergence of a paradigm, embodied in the published works of one or more great scientists, defining and exemplifying the concepts and methods of research appropriate to the study of a certain class of natural phenomena and serving as an inspiration to further research by its promise of success in explaining those phenomena.
3. A period of normal science conducted within a conceptual and methodological framework derived from the paradigmatic achievement, involving actualization of the promise of success, further articulation of the paradigm, exploration of the possibilities within the paradigm, use of existing theory to predict facts, solving of scientific puzzles, development of new applications of theory, and the like.
4. A crisis stage of varying duration precipitated by the

discovery of natural phenomena that "violate the paradigm-induced expectations that govern normal science" and marked by the invention of new theories designed to take account of the anomalous facts.

5. A relatively abrupt transition to a new paradigm brought about by the achievements of a scientific genius who defines and exemplifies a new conceptual and methodological framework incommensurable with the old.

6. Continuation of normal science within the new paradigm.

Professor Kuhn's examples of the formation and transformation of paradigms are drawn entirely from the history of the physical sciences, but he gives us no reason to believe that his analysis is not applicable to the sciences generally. It may be worthwhile, therefore, to examine the developments leading up to the Darwinian revolution in natural history to see to what extent they fit the pattern of historical development described in Kuhn's book.

Perhaps the best way to begin the investigation is to ask: When did natural history first acquire a paradigm? When did it arrive at a state characterized by "research firmly based upon one or more past scientific achievements that some particular scientific community acknowledged for a time as supplying the foundation for its further practice"; achievements "sufficiently unprecedented to attract an enduring group of adherents away from competing modes of scientific activity," yet "sufficiently open-ended to leave all sorts of problems for the redefined group of practitioners to resolve"?

This is not an easy question to answer. On the whole, however, it seems that such a condition cannot be said to have prevailed in natural history until the emergence of systematic natural history in the late seventeenth century, its embodiment in the publications of John Ray and Joseph Pitton de Tournefort, and its apotheosis in the works of Carl Linnaeus.

Aristotle and Theophrastus had laid the foundations of scientific zoology and botany two thousand years earlier, but their achievements cannot be said to have given rise to a continuing tradition of research based on their precept and example. The herbalists cannot be said to have been continuing the Theophrastian tradition, nor can Pliny, Albertus Magnus, Gesner, and Aldrovandi be said to have been the continuators of Aristotle in the same sense that Brisson, Jussieu, Candolle, Cuvier, Lamarck, Hooker, and Agassiz were continuators of the tradition established by Tournefort, Ray, and Linnaeus. Doubtless the Aristotelian achievement was profounder, broader, and in some ways more fecund than that of the founders of systematic natural history, but it did not, like theirs, give rise to and dominate an enduring tradition of scientific research of the kind Kuhn has in mind when he speaks of normal science.

It may be objected, however, that systematic natural history as practiced by Ray, Tournefort, and Linnaeus, was not a science in Kuhn's terms because it did not explain anything, but only named, classified, and described natural objects. This objection raises the difficult problem whether science can be defined in absolute terms; that is, in such a way that the definition is valid for all sciences in all periods of history.

Kuhn himself seems to favor a loose, relativistic concept of science that would allow for the fact that every great scientific revolution involves some redefinition of the nature and aim of science. He tells us that no man is a scientist unless he is "concerned to understand the world and to extend the precision and scope with which it has been ordered." On the other hand, he stresses the importance of respecting "the historical integrity of that [older] science in its own time." With respect to the acceptance and rejection of paradigms he asserts that "there is no standard higher than the assent of the relevant community," and he rejects flatly the view, which he attributes to Charles Gillispie, that "the history of science records a continuing increase in the maturity and refinement of man's conception of the nature of science."

It would seem, therefore, that whatever the ultimate truth about the nature of science may be, no objection to the scientific status of systematic natural history can be drawn from Kuhn's book. Systematic natural historians were concerned to understand the world and to extend the precision and scope with which it was ordered. They considered themselves scientists and were so considered by their contemporaries, including the physical scientists. True, they did not consider it their business as natural historians to explain the origin of species, but neither did Newton consider it his business as a natural philosopher to explain the origin of the solar system.

Like Newton, Ray and Linnaeus took for granted a static concept of nature that regarded all the structures of nature as created and wisely designed by an omnipotent God in the beginning. This assumption of the permanence and wise design of specific forms and of the basic structures of nature generally was an essential feature of the paradigm of systematic natural history, integrally related to the belief that the aim of natural history was to name, classify, and describe.

By every criterion laid down by Kuhn there was a paradigm of systematic natural history. Emerging from the scientific achievements of Ray, Tournefort, and Linnaeus, it involved commitments on all the levels—cosmological, epistemological, methodological, and others—mentioned by Kuhn. Embodied in manuals and popularizations, articulated with increasing precision, communicated by precept and example, celebrated in prose and verse, it dominated the field of natural history for nearly two hundred years and helped to prepare the way for a far different, far more dynamic kind of natural history. To this extent, then, we can say that Kuhn's model of scientific development seems to fit fairly well with what is known concerning the emergence of systematic natural history as a science of nature.

Having established, at least to our own satisfaction, that natural history first acquired a paradigm in the Kuhnian sense through the work of Ray, Tournefort, and Linnaeus, we next inquire when this paradigm may be said to have been supplanted by a different one. Here it seems generally agreed that the publication of Charles Darwin's *Origin of Species* was the decisive event in the transition from a static, taxonomy-oriented natural history to a dynamic and causal evolutionary biology. Whatever the exact nature and causes of the Darwinian revolution, there can be little doubt that Darwin's work inaugurated a new era in the study of organic nature. Before discussing this revolution further, however, it will be well to inquire into its genesis in order to discover whether the development of natural history from Linnaeus to Darwin followed the pattern of normal science, anomaly, crisis, and paradigm invention described by Kuhn.

At the outset of this inquiry we are confronted with a phenomenon for which Kuhn's model makes no provision, namely, the appearance of a counter-paradigm coeval, or nearly so, with the establishment of the static paradigm of natural history.

In the same mid-eighteenth-century years when Linnaeus was rearing the edifice of systematic natural history on foundations laid by Ray and Tournefort, the Count de Buffon was publishing his splendid *Histoire Naturelle, Générale et Particulière*, based on a profoundly different concept of natural history from that which inspired Linnaeus and his forerunners. In Linnaeus' view, the function of the natural historian was to name, classify, and describe the productions of the earth and, above all, to search for a natural method of classification. In Buffon's opinion, classifications were arbitrary human devices that played a useful but subordinate role in the main business of natural history, which was to explain the observed uniformities in nature's productions as necessary results of the operations of the hidden system of laws, elements, and forces constituting primary, active, and causative nature. Where Linnaeus saw a world of plants and animals neatly ordered and perfectly adapted to their surroundings by the wise design of an omnipotent Creator, Buffon saw a confused array of living forms, some better adapted to their environment than others, all subject to modification through changes in climate, diet, and the general circumstances of life, all threatened in one degree or another by the activities of man and by the gradual cooling of the earth that had spawned these beings by its own powers. While Linnaeus described and catalogued species, genera, orders, and classes, searching for the natural method of classification (presumably one corresponding to a pattern in the mind of the Creator), Buffon devoted his energies to studying the processes of generation, inheritance, and variation by which various kinds of animals had been produced and modified.

Like Darwin a century later, Buffon investigated the history of domesticated plants and animals and discovered the importance of artificial selection, both conscious and unconscious, in producing domestic races. He conducted experiments in animal hybridization. He compared the quadrupeds of the Old World with those of the New, and sought to understand their similarities and differences as effects of descent with modification. He collected and compared fossils from Europe, Asia, and America and attempted to envisage the epochs of earth history in the light of these discoveries. He canvassed the literature concerning human races, manlike apes, wild children, pygmies, and giants, and strove to portray the history of man as a part of the wider history of nature. Finally, like Darwin, he invented a theory of pangenesis to explain the apparent facts of heredity, growth, nutrition, and modification through environmental change.

In all of this there was much that was speculative, much that was tentative and incomplete. But the challenge to Linnaean precept and practice in natural history was clear and unmistakable. Buffon had promulgated and in a great degree exemplified a new kind of natural history: dynamic, causal, nonteleological, time-oriented, uniformitarian in principle if not always in practice, concerned with discovering the laws and mechanisms of organic change, aimed ultimately at control of nature through an understanding of her modes of operation. The difference in outlook between the new natural history and the old is apparent in the two following quotations:

> *Linnaeus:* The study of natural history, simple, beautiful, and instructive, consists in the collection, arrangement, and exhibition of the various productions of the earth.

> *Buffon:* In general, kindred of species is one of those mysteries of Nature, which man can never unravel, without a long continued and difficult series of experiments. . . . Is the ass more allied to the horse than the zebra? Does the wolf approach nearer to the dog than the fox or jackal? At what distance from man shall we place the large apes, who resemble him so perfectly in conformation of body? Are all the species of animals the same now that they

were originally? . . . . Have not the feeble species been destroyed by the stronger, or by the tyranny of man. . . . Does not a race, like a mixed species, proceed from an anomalous individual which forms the original stock? How many questions does this subject admit of; and how few of them are we in a condition to solve? How many facts must be discovered before we can even form probable conjectures?[1]

It appears, then, that natural history acquired *two* paradigms in rapid succession in the mid-eighteenth century, the Linnaean and the Buffonian, and that these paradigms were diametrically opposed in spirit, presuppositions, and concept of scientific method. The first, blending Aristotelian logic and teleology with a static form of the Christian doctrine of creation, identified natural history with taxonomy. The second, deriving from the Cartesian vision of nature as a self-contained system of matter in motion, sought to gain insight into this hidden system of nature by observing uniformities in the effects it produced and constructing models capable of explaining the observed effects as necessary consequences of the operations of the system.

The Buffonian paradigm was *not* a response to anomalies and contradictions within the Linnaean paradigm. Instead, it was a conscious attempt to introduce into natural history concepts derived from natural philosophy, from the seventeenth-century revolution in physics and cosmology. Buffon had had excellent training in mathematical physics and had played a significant role in the introduction of Newtonian ideas on the Continent. In his theory of generation he made an explicit analogy between his own organic molecules and the atoms of Newton, between his own internal molds and the force of gravitation.

But, despite these Newtonian analogies, Buffon was more Cartesian than Newtonian in his approach to nature. For him the uniformities observable in the motions of the planets were not, as Newton supposed, evidences of the Creator's wise design. Instead, they were a challenge to the natural philosopher to imagine a previous state of the system of matter in motion from which the solar system might have been formed by the operation of the Newtonian laws of motion. Likewise, the uniformities that comparative anatomy discerned in the organization of animals were not to be interpreted as evidences of design or manifestations of some transcendental idea, but rather as occasions for constructing a theory of generation that would display these uniformities as necessary products of the motions of organic molecules. Descartes and Leibniz, not Newton, were the sources of Buffon's paradigm of natural history.

How, then, are we to interpret the development of natural history from the death of Linnaeus (1778) and Buffon (1788) to the publication of Darwin's *Origin of Species*? Did the Linnaean paradigm predominate, develop internal contradictions and crises, and then give way to a new paradigm that had no history save the history of its development in the mind of Charles Darwin? Or did the Buffonian paradigm develop alongside the Linnaean paradigm, gradually claiming more converts until it found a decisive champion in Darwin? Or was there some interaction between the two paradigms, a thesis-antithesis relationship that eventually produced a Darwinian synthesis? Unfortunately, we know too little about the development of natural history in the nineteenth century to generalize with confidence on this subject, but it may help to consider various hypotheses in the light of what we do know.

When we examine the development of natural history in the period 1788–1859, we discover striking differences in theoretical approach to the data of natural history on both the individual and the national level. Kuhn gives us very little guidance in this kind of situation. In *The Structure of Scientific Revolutions* he treats the evolution of scientific thought and technique as if it were impervious to the influence of national cultural traditions. In another work, however, he argues that *Naturphilosophie* played a significant role in the genesis of the principle of the conservation of energy, and *Naturphilosophie* was a peculiarly German phenomenon.[2]

As will be seen, *Naturphilosophie* gave rise to something approaching a counter-paradigm in natural history in the early nineteenth century. Theories of natural selection seem to have been a purely British phenomenon in the same period. Apparently what is "normal" for the scientists of one country may be exotic from the point of view of another cultural tradition, and the cross-fertilization of ideas generated in different national contexts may play an important role in the development of scientific theory. For these reasons, as well as for the sake of convenience, we shall proceed country by country in our consideration of nineteenth-century developments in natural history.

We begin with France and the Museum of Natural History, the largest, best-subsidized, best-organized, best-equipped establishment for the study of natural history in the world. Here, if anywhere, we should learn how a mature science develops. If we confine our attention to certain eminent figures at the museum, notably A. L. de Jussieu and Georges Cuvier, we can make the Kuhnian model work without undue difficulty.

Building on the earlier work of Tournefort, Ray, Linnaeus, and his uncle Bernard de Jussieu, A. L. de Jussieu devised a system of botanical classification, the "natural system," which gradually gained acceptance in France, Switzerland, the Germanies, England, and America as the nineteenth century progressed. In zoology Cuvier revolutionized taxonomy by basing it squarely on comparative anatomy, Aristotelian functionalism, and Jussieu's principle of the subordination of characters. But this revolution, far from overthrowing the static paradigm of natural history, served only to strengthen and further articulate the taxonomic, teleological approach to natural history. Cuvier was proclaimed the Aristotle of the nineteenth century; his influence radiated throughout Western science.

At the same time, Cuvier dealt successfully with a major anomaly that emerged from his own researches, namely, the apparent fact that many species had become extinct. It is hard for us today to realize how anomalous this fact was for the naturalists of the eighteenth and early nineteenth centuries. In the static paradigm of natural history species had been defined as part of the stable framework of creation: "the Works created by God at first, and by him conserved to this Day in the same State and Condition in which they were first made."[3] It was inconceivable, therefore, that a species could become extinct. "For if one link in nature's chain might be lost," wrote Jefferson, "another and another might be lost, till this whole system of things should vanish piecemeal. . . ."[4]

Naturalists were extremely reluctant to envisage the possibility that species could perish, but by Cuvier's time the evidence to that effect had become overwhelming. Cuvier's work on the organic remains of the Paris basin removed the last vestige of doubt. The static paradigm of natural history was now confronted with a major anomaly demanding explanation.

It is a tribute to Cuvier's genius that he achieved a resolution of the crisis precipitated by his own researches. By extending the method and principles of comparative anatomy to the study of organic remains, he simultaneously demonstrated the differences between living and fossil species and brought the latter within the domain of systematic natural history. At the same time, by adopting the geological catastrophism of Jean Deluc, he preserved the main features of the static paradigm. Species might become extinct as a result of dramatic geological upheavals of unknown origin, but in the intervals between these upheavals permanence and wise design reigned supreme, providing a stable framework for retrospective taxonomy.

By means of the doctrine of successive creations, which emerged from the researches of Cuvier, Parkinson, Buckland, and others, the static paradigm was given a new lease on life. This method of saving a paradigm by a compromise solution deserves fuller attention from Kuhn. Tycho Brahe's theory of the heavens is an earlier example of the same phenomenon.

On Kuhnian principles we should presumably look to further developments within the redefined static paradigm for the anomalies and crises that gave rise to Darwin's counter-paradigm. But the subsequent development of the "natural system" in botany and of Cuvierian ideas in zoology and paleontology failed to produce a crisis in systematic natural history. George Bentham's account of the development of botany in the first six decades of the nineteenth century is a tale of the progressive triumph of the "natural system," undisturbed by more than fleeting misgivings about the theoretical foundations of the system.[5] In zoology the chief successors of Cuvier were Owen and Agassiz, and although both showed a tendency toward contamination by *Naturphilosophie*, neither ever doubted the essential soundness of the basic tenets of the static paradigm of natural history.

During the same half century, however, evolutionary concepts were slowly gathering momentum. From what source did they spring if not from difficulties encountered within the Linnaean-Cuvierian paradigm of *nommer, classer et décrire*? Strange to say (and this is a fact difficult to fit into the Kuhnian model), the chief source of evolutionary ideas in France during the period was the tradition of interpreting nature as a law-bound system of matter in motion, of which Buffon had been the chief exponent in the eighteenth century.

Although Cuvier established the static paradigm as the main tradition at the Museum of Natural History, the ghost of Buffon was never completely exorcised from the institution he had raised to greatness. In 1800, immediately after the death of the venerable Daubenton (to whom Buffon's ideas were anathema), Lacépède and Lamarck both published evolutionary speculations similar in outlook to those of their mentor Buffon. Twenty-five years later Étienne Geoffroy St. Hilaire, having already fallen afoul of Cuvier by his advocacy of transcendental anatomy, turned to evolutionary speculations of a distinctly Buffonian character. Indeed, one of his last publications contained an appreciation of Buffon.[6]

Concerning Lacépède's evolutionism little need be said, since Lacépède was soon drawn away from natural history into the Napoleonic administration, where, unlike Cuvier, he found little time for scientific research.[7]

Lamarck, on the contrary, was a major figure in the development of scientific natural history. Trained by Bernard de Jussieu, befriended by Buffon (whose son he tutored), Lamarck made a sufficient reputation as a botanist to be appointed to the chair of invertebrate zoology at the Museum of Natural History. There, less than ten years after his appointment, he sketched the outlines of a general "physics of the earth," embracing "all the primary considerations of the earth's atmosphere, of the characteristics and continual changes of the earth's external crust, and finally of the origin and development of living organisms." The first part of this science he called Meteorology, the second Hydrogeology, and the third Biology. Biology, he explained, was not to concern itself primarily with taxonomy, but rather with discovering the causes, laws, and direction of organic change.

How are we to regard Lamarck's effort to redefine the basic concepts and goals of natural history? From a Kuhnian point of view this was certainly an attempt at a scientific revolution affecting every level of natural history from the concept of a species to the definition of the ultimate goals of the naturalist. It had all the characteristics of a scientific revolution except success.

Unfortunately, Kuhn's analysis lays down no guidelines for dealing with unsuccessful revolutions in science. We cannot deny that Lamarck's ideas were revolutionary. In broad outline—geological uniformitarianism with its vast time scheme, descent with modification by natural causes, progressive development up to and including man, the search for the laws and causes of organic change—they were similar to the ideas Darwin was to champion half a century later. But the proposed mechanism of organic change was unconvincing, and the circumstantial evidence supporting the theory was scanty and sporadic.

Yet one feels entitled to ask why this revolution should have been attempted at this time. Was there an anomaly-generated crisis in natural history in the late eighteenth century which gave rise to Lamarck's counter-paradigm and the less fully articulated counter-paradigms of Erasmus Darwin, Lacépède, and others? It is hard to believe that any such crisis existed at that time. Evidence indicating widespread extinction of species did not become available until *after* Lamarck had arrived at the grand outlines of his theory, and, in any case, Lamarck did not believe that species became extinct. (So-called extinct species were for him simply the ancestors of living forms.) Likewise it seems unlikely that some anomaly or crisis in botanical or zoological taxonomy drove Lamarck to an evolutionary position, although Charles Lyell was later to ascribe Lamarck's evolutionism to the difficulties he encountered in distinguishing species from varieties.

On the whole, it seems more likely that Lamarck became convinced of the mutability of organic forms from his geological researches, and that he guessed the direction of organic change partly from the old idea of the scale of nature and partly from the researches of Jussieu and Cuvier on the anatomy of plants and animals.

Like Buffon, Lamarck started from the idea that nature was a law-bound system of matter in motion. But, whereas Buffon attributed the main features of the earth's surface to the action of tidal currents operating on the plastic surface of a cooling globe, Lamarck invoked the action of running water and the progressive displacement of ocean basins by the action of waves. As a result, he adopted a time scheme of millions of years for earth history in place of the tens of thousands envisaged by Buffon. Nature, he declared, had plenty of time and circumstances at her disposal, and everything conspired to prove that all of her works, even the largest and most imposing, were subject to slow change.

Thus, Lamarck drew from a thoroughgoing geological uniformitarianism the inevitable conclusion that organic forms were mutable. In the static paradigm of natural history inorganic, organic, and human history were assumed to be synchronous. The basic structures of inorganic nature were thought to have been perfectly contrived by the Creator to subserve the needs of the higher levels of existence, animate and rational. But if Lamarck and Hutton were right, if the inorganic environment had been undergoing constant slow change for millions and millions of years as a result of geological processes governed by the general laws of physics and chemistry, with no vestige of a beginning, no prospect of an end, then the organisms inhabiting the globe must have changed too, or they would have suffered extinction.

Thus the first serious crisis in the static paradigm of natural history arose, not within the system of naming, classifying, and describing, which constituted the heart and soul of the paradigm, but rather from a postulate affecting the wider framework of assumptions concerning the stability of the visible structures of nature and their hierarchical ordering with respect to each other. Being geologists rather than naturalists, Hutton and Playfair did not develop the implications of geological uniformitarianism for systematic natural history. But Lamarck could not escape them. Either he must accept the wholesale extinction of species as a logical consequence of his geological ideas, or he must conceive the organisms inhabiting the earth's surface as being endowed with a natural capacity to undergo the changes required for survival amid changing circumstances and seek to discover the means by which these changes had been effected.

Of these two alternatives Lamarck chose the latter, invoking use and disuse as the chief agencies of organic change. His next task was to explore the implications of his revolutionary hypothesis for taxonomy and the idea of a natural method of classification. Here Lamarck seems to have taken his clue from the old idea of the scale of nature. In any case, he devoted his energies chiefly to working out a classification that would reflect the path nature had followed in giving birth to progressively more complicated living forms.

It appears, then, that Lamarck's counter-paradigm sprang more from a predisposition toward a uniformitarian view of nature's operations than from a sense of difficulties to be resolved in the structure of systematic natural history. This is not to say that Lamarck did not find the evolutionary postulate useful in taxonomy, but only that taxonomic problems were probably not the main source of his belief in the mutability of species.[8]

However that may be, the question remains as to what role, if any, Lamarck's theory played in the eventual emergence of the Darwinian counter-paradigm. It is fashionable nowadays to deny Lamarck any status as a precursor of Darwin, but we had best postpone this question of the influence of Lamarck's *révolution manqué* on Darwin's *révolution véritable* until we deal with developments in Britain. Suffice it to say for the moment that Lamarck's ideas haunted natural history during the first half of the nineteenth century much as the spectre of communism haunted social theory in the second half. Darwin himself once referred to Lamarck as "the Hutton of geology," obviously intending to write "the Hutton of biology." That was a high compliment and a shrewd characterization. In extending the uniformitarian concept from geology to biology Lamarck foreshadowed the doom of the static paradigm of natural history.

Before turning to developments in Britain that proved decisive for the overthrow of the static paradigm, we must consider briefly another attempt at revolutionizing the conceptual framework of natural history, namely, the attempt associated with the rise of German *Naturphilosophie*. Although Goethe, Oken, Carus, and their followers did not break with the main tradition of systematic natural history as sharply as Lamarck did, their deviation from some of its basic tenets approached the dimensions of a genuine counter-paradigm and gave rise to a kind of evolutionism.

Naturphilosophie diverged from the Linnaean-Cuvierian tradition in natural history in several important respects.

1. It rejected the teleological functionalism of the dominant tradition in favor of a science of pure form, in which form was conceived as dictating function, not function form. The Cuvierian techniques in comparative anatomy were retained, but they were employed for a new purpose: the discovery of a uniform plan of organization pervading the organic world. Instead of the correlation of parts and their adaptation to each other and to the conditions of existence, the watchwords of transcendental anatomy were unity of plan and the correspondence of parts. Classification was still important, but it was subordinated to the search for archetypes.

2. Emphasis on development, on nature begetting, supplanted the traditional preoccupation with the description and classification of begotten forms. On the whole, the idea of development was restricted to embryological development, but embryological study led on to the idea of parallelisms between the levels of organization traversed in embryological development and the levels

of organization revealed by comparative anatomy and, eventually, by the fossil record. By some writers these parallelisms were given an evolutionary interpretation.

3. Creationism was muted or abandoned outright in favor of pantheistic ideas of creative nature, spontaneous generation, and the like. Whereas in England most naturalists considered belief in spontaneous generation unscientific and atheistical, many German writers considered the doctrine of successive creations unscientific, preferring to resort to successive spontaneous generations to explain the changes in flora and fauna revealed in the fossil record.

How are we to regard these developments in the light of Kuhn's model? Was this another abortive revolution provoked by anomalous discoveries in systematic natural history? Such an interpretation would be hard to sustain. *Naturphilosophie* was an outgrowth of German idealistic philosophy. Perhaps it developed in reaction to certain aspects of the thought of the Enlightenment, as Charles Gillispie has suggested. But do we solve the problem of how science develops by casting whole scientific movements into the outer darkness with the label "subjective science" attached to them?

Naturphilosophie enlisted many able scientists under its banner. Its influence was felt throughout Europe, even in England, where Richard Owen became its leading exponent. In France, Étienne Geoffroy St. Hilaire elaborated a science of pure form independently of the German writers, and Geoffroy can scarcely be described as anti-Enlightenment. Shall we not rather say that the idea of an all-embracing unity of plan in the organic world was a natural and legitimate product of scientific imagination seeking ever wider generality in its ordering of nature?

But here again, as in the case of the very different visions of nature and natural science promulgated by Buffon and Lamarck, paradigm construction did not wait on the emergence of anomalies and crises in systematic natural history. On the contrary, it ran ahead of known facts, postulating a wider unity in nature than could be demonstrated and delving into the study of embryological development in search of confirming data.

In the end, the devotees of transcendental anatomy failed to establish their case. But their researches and many of their concepts, such as the ideas of homology, recapitulation, balancement, and even evolution, entered into the general fund of knowledge and speculation available to Darwin and his contemporaries.

We come now to Britain, where the main revolution in natural history was to take place, although from an unexpected quarter. Systematic natural history made slow progress in Britain after the brilliant work of John Ray in the late seventeenth century. Linnaean influence did not become entrenched there until the 1780s, when Sir James Edward Smith acquired a vested interest in Linnaean botany through his purchase of Linnaeus's herbarium, books, and letters and joined with the Reverend Samuel Goodenough and others in founding the Linnaean Society of London. In zoology, George Shaw adopted the Linnaean classification in preference to Thomas Pennant's system based on Ray.

As the nineteenth century wore on, British science responded to developments on the Continent and began to make solid contributions to the literature of natural history. In botany the so-called natural system of Jussieu and Candolle was gradually introduced by Robert Brown, John Lindley, George Bentham, and the Hookers, and Kew Gardens began to emerge as a center for the study of world botany. In zoology the dominant figure was Richard Owen, who combined Cuvier's techniques in comparative anatomy with the transcendental ideas of Oken, Goethe, and Geoffroy St. Hilaire in a way that would have dismayed Cuvier.

There was nothing very revolutionary in all this, nor does one sense a spirit of unrest or crisis among these naturalists. In Bentham's eyes the period before Darwin was characterized by the progressive triumph of the "natural system," leading many botanists to think that little was left for systematic botany but mopping up operations Joseph Dalton Hooker was privy to Darwin's subversive hypothesis from

1844 on, but Darwin's powerful ideas worked slowly on Hooker's imagination. Apart from his intercourse with Darwin, Hooker would never have broken out of the static paradigm of natural history. In zoology there was equally little evidence of a crisis psychology. The *Transactions* of the Zoological Society of London and the periodic progress reports of the British Association for the Advancement of Science gave little hint of the coming revolution. True, there was an extraordinary outcry against *The Vestiges of the Natural History of Creation*, but Chambers's book was a challenge from outside the natural history establishment, not from within.[9]

What, then, were the sources of the British revolution in natural history, if they are not to be found in the internal development of systematic botany and zoology? One might be tempted to find them in the eighteenth-century tradition of speculative philosophy of nature represented by Erasmus Darwin, but Erasmus Darwin's scientific impact, as distinguished from his popular influence, was negligible. Of far greater consequence for the evolution of natural history were certain developments in British geology and political economy in the years from 1775 to 1835.

Let us speak first of the progress of geology. The immediate impact of Hutton's uniformitarianism on systematic natural history was minimal, partly because his ideas were not widely accepted, but also because neither Hutton nor Playfair made more than passing reference to the organic remains embedded in the crust of the earth. Nevertheless, as we have seen in our discussion of Lamarck, geological uniformitarianism had momentous implications for the doctrine of the fixity of species. These implications were not lost on Playfair, as can be seen in the following passage from his *Illustrations of the Huttonian Theory of the Earth*, a passage used by Lyell as a motto for the second volume of his *Principles*:

> The inhabitants of the globe, then, like all the other parts of it, are subject to change: It is not only the individual that perishes, but whole *species*, and even perhaps *genera*, are extinguished. . . . But besides this, a change in the animal kingdom seems to be a part of the order of nature, and is visible in instances to which human power cannot have extended.[10]

For the time being, however, British naturalists and pale-ontologists evaded the issues posed by geological uniformitarianism in the same way that Cuvier evaded them in France. They rejected uniformitarianism in favor of a theory of successive creations and extinctions and devoted themselves to naming, classifying, and describing the organic remains of former worlds and to discovering how to identify and correlate geological formations by means of them. In so doing they unwittingly set the stage for Charles Lyell's revolutionary extension of the uniformitarian doctrine to organic phenomena.

There is little evidence, however, that Lyell's great book was a response to a state of crisis in geological science. Instead, it seems to have been conceived as a reaffirmation of uniformitarian principles, and, what was crucial for the development of evolutionary ideas, an extension of them to the organic world, at least in regard to the extinction of species. Lyell's shift to a dynamic and causal view of organic nature is apparent in the opening paragraph of his *Principles*, where he says: "Geology is the science which investigates the successive changes that have taken place in the organic and inorganic kingdoms of nature; it inquires into the causes of these changes, and the influence which they have exerted in modifying the surface and external structure of our planet. By these researches . . . we acquire a more perfect knowledge of its present condition, and more comprehensive views concerning the laws now governing its animate and inanimate productions."[11] Lamarck himself could not have asked for a better statement of the aims and outlook of a comprehensive science of the earth and its productions.

But Lyell was not prepared to follow Lamarck down the uniformitarian path to a full-blown evolutionism. Like Lamarck, he drew from geological uniformitarianism the conclusion that plant and animal species must change with changing circumstances or perish. But, whereas Lamarck viewed organisms as endowed with an innate capacity to undergo the changes necessary for survival, Lyell, unconvinced that organisms possessed an unlimited capacity for variation, chose instead to envisage piecemeal extinction of species as the eventual consequence of their limited ability to adapt to changed conditions. Thus, whereas Lamarck's energies were directed toward imagining the processes by which organisms adapted to changing circumstances and toward tracing the path of their upward evolution, Lyell's were concentrated on studying the effects of environmental changes on the chances of survival of species possessing limited powers of variation. Not evolution, but elimination in the struggle for survival, became the focus of his attention so far as species were concerned.

This was precisely the direction of thought that was to eventuate in the theory of natural selection. Moreover, it was a mode of thinking that came naturally to Englishmen, steeped as they were in the tradition of Adam Smith, Malthus, and Ricardo. Surely it is no mere coincidence that all of the men who arrived at some idea of natural selection in the first half of the nineteenth century—one thinks of William Wells, Patrick Matthew, Charles Lyell, Edward Blyth, Charles Darwin, A. R. Wallace, and Herbert Spencer—were British. Here, if anywhere in the history of science, we have a striking example of the influence of national habits of thought on the development of scientific theory, a phenomenon difficult to reconcile with Kuhn's internalist approach. For the cast of mind we have been describing affected not merely the timing of the revolution in natural history but its central concept, the idea of competition, survival of the fittest, and consequent progress.

Lyell himself stopped short of a theory of the origin of species, falling back on the traditional belief in special creation and wise design. But his uniformitarian explanation of the piecemeal extinction of species seemed to cry out for a correlative explanation of the origin of species by natural causes. The elements of a non-Lamarckian theory of evolution, stressing the struggle for existence and survival of the fittest, were present in his work cheek by jowl with his systematic exposition and discussion of the Lamarckian alternative to his own steady-state concept of earth history. Little wonder, then, that Lyell's *Principles* provided the impetus for evolutionary speculation in Britain from the time of its publication onward.

Chambers and Spencer, impressed more by Lyell's exposition of Lamarckian ideas than by his refutation of them, chose Lamarck's kind of evolutionism. Darwin and Wallace, aware of the inadequacy of Lamarck's theory of organic change but convinced of the essential truth of transmutationism, set out to discover the mechanism of change. Meanwhile, systematic natural history continued on its accustomed course, untroubled by any sense of crisis. A revolution was impending, but it was to come from outside, not from within, the establishment.

We come now to Darwin and the revolution in natural history associated with his name and achievements. From Kuhn's hypothesis we should expect this revolution to be noncumulative in character and to involve the substitution of a new paradigm of natural history incommensurable with the static paradigm that had reigned before the revolution. The first question, then, is: Was the Darwinian revolution noncumulative in character? That is, did it break sharply with the concepts, methods, and modes of thought that had prevailed before 1859?

From what has already been said it should be apparent that this question does not admit of a simple yes or no answer. If we compare Darwin's ideas and methods with those that had prevailed in the main tradition of systematic natural history, namely, the tradition of Linnaeus, Jussieu, Candolle, Cuvier, Owen, and Agassiz, we discover a profound break with the past, though *not* one generated in response to internal difficulties in the tradition that was overthrown.

If, on the other hand, we compare Darwin's concepts and methods with those of Buffon, Erasmus Darwin, Lamarck, Étienne Geoffroy St. Hilaire, and Charles Lyell, we begin to have doubts about the noncumulative character of the Darwinian revolution. We discover that some aspects of Darwin's thought and practice were more original than others.

Darwin himself made no claim to have invented the idea of

organic evolution. He was too well acquainted with the writings of Lamarck, Geoffroy St. Hilaire, and his own grandfather, Erasmus Darwin, all of whom he had read or reread on his return from the voyage of the *Beagle*, to make any such claim. He claimed only to have discovered "the means of modification and co-adaptation" in nature and thereby to have transformed a speculative idea of descent with modification into a workable theory of the origin of species. To this he might have added that he had done more than merely hit upon the idea of natural selection as the means of modification and co-adaptation. More important, he had deduced the consequences of his hypothesis and endeavored to show by observation and experiment that they actually obtained in nature. This combination of inductive and deductive methods had long prevailed in the physical sciences, but Darwin was the first to apply it systematically in natural history. His methods were as revolutionary as his theory.

Thus, one's judgment as to the cumulative or noncumulative character of the Darwinian revolution depends largely on whether one stresses the general concept of descent with modification or the particular theory of natural selection as the means of organic modification in nature. The general concept had a history reaching back at least to Buffon. Indeed, Thomas Henry Huxley was inclined to credit Descartes with insight into what Huxley deemed "the fundamental proposition of Evolution," namely, that "the whole world, living and not living, is the result of the mutual interaction, according to definite laws, of the forces possessed by the molecules of which the primitive nebulosity of the universe was composed."[12] In one sense Huxley was right. Geological uniformitarianism and its corollary of indefinite mutability in the organic world were implied in the Cartesian program of deriving the present structures of nature from a simpler, more homogeneous state of the system of matter in motion by the operation of the laws of nature. The drawing out of this implication by Buffon, Lamarck, Lyell, and others sprang more from the appeal of this vision of nature and natural science to imaginative minds than it did from factual discoveries, which could always be interpreted differently by less imaginative observers.

Darwin himself conceded the importance of this dynamic and causal approach to nature when he wrote in 1863: "Whether the naturalist believes in the views given by Lamarck, by Geoffroy St. Hilaire, by the author of the 'Vestiges,' by Mr. Wallace or by myself, signifies extremely little in comparison with the admission that species have descended from other species, and have not been created immutable: for he who admits this as a great truth has a wide field opened to him for further inquiry."[13]

The difficulty was, however, that there could be no general acceptance of the idea that species have descended from species until someone could show convincingly *how* this could take place. The revolution in natural history had been prophesied for more than a century, but the fulfillment of the prophecy had to wait on the discovery and elaboration of a theory of natural selection. It was Darwin and Wallace who achieved this result, but, as we have seen, the way was cleared for them by Charles Lyell and by the British school of political economy. Patrick Matthew, Edward Blyth, and Herbert Spencer were products of the same climate of opinion.

Yet, curiously enough, although the theory of natural selection played an indispensable role in converting the scientific world to an evolutionary point of view, many who accepted transmutationism after Darwin rejected natural selection as the key to organic evolution. Neo-Lamarckian evolutionists, some of them distinguished scientists, were numerous in the late nineteenth century.

This fact brings us to the final question, whether Darwin's work effectively established a new paradigm incommensurable with the static paradigm of systematic natural history. If by establishing a new paradigm we mean simply establishing an evolutionary point of view in biology, Darwin certainly did that, and the new point of view can justly be described as incommensurable with the Linnaean paradigm, although no more incommensurable with it than the point of view of

Buffon or Lamarck was. If, on the other hand, we mean that Darwin's work established the theory of natural selection and Darwin's general assumptions and methods as the norm of scientific thought and practice among biologists, this is a more dubious proposition.

As we have seen, many scientists accepted Darwin's evolutionism but not his emphasis on natural selection. Among systematists, moreover, although lip service was now paid to the Lamarckian and Darwinian idea that the natural method of classification was one that reflected phylogeny, taxonomic methods were slow to change. The anthropologists, far from following Darwin's lead in investigating the origin of human races, settled down to three-quarters of a century of hairsplitting racial taxonomy. As for Darwin's ideas on the subject of heredity and variation, they did give rise to a school of English geneticists led by Galton, Pearson, and Weldon. But, far from being generally accepted, these ideas were attacked strenuously by Weismann and others and were eventually overthrown by the rediscovery of Mendel's laws and the development of cytology. In fact, it could be argued that nothing approaching a "Darwinian" paradigm became established until the 1930s, and even that paradigm was Darwinian only in a very loose sense.

We conclude as follows:

1. Through the work of Ray, Tournefort, and Linnaeus natural history acquired a conceptual framework that dominated the study of natural history until Darwin published his *Origin of Species*, after which systematics was gradually reshaped and relocated within the broader framework of evolutionary biology.

2. Challenges to the dominance of the Linnaean framework in natural history arose both within and outside of that framework.

3. The challenges arising within the static view of nature and natural history failed to precipitate a search for new premises; they were either ignored or evaded by compromises such as the theory of successive creations.

4. Rival concepts, such as those propounded by Buffon, Lamarck, and the transcendental anatomists, arose from time to time, but not in response to anomalies or crises within the dominant view. These counter-concepts exerted a significant influence both on the static view of nature and on the developments that were to eventuate in its overthrow.

5. The evolutionary alternative to the static outlook developed chiefly outside the Linnaean framework in the form of a search for a science of nature that would derive the phenomena of nature from the operations of a law-bound system of matter in motion. The earliest and most powerful challenge to the static view of nature was the challenge implied in geological uniformitarianism. It was this postulate, rather than particular scientific discoveries, that drove Lamarck to an evolutionary position and led Lyell to envisage the piecemeal extinction of species through the struggle for existence.

6. The eventual emergence of the theory of natural selection in Britain seems to have owed a great deal to the influence of the competitive ethos that pervaded British political economy and British mores generally.

7. The Darwinian revolution displayed elements both of continuity and discontinuity with the past. It overthrew the static view of nature and natural history but failed to establish a clear-cut paradigm in its place.

8. The Kuhnian paradigm of paradigms can be made to fit certain aspects of the development of natural history from Ray to Darwin, but its adequacy as a conceptual model for that development seems doubtful. The use of Kuhnian terminology in this essay should not be interpreted as implying belief in its general utility for the historiography of science. At the same time, it should be remembered that an inadequate hypothesis is better than none at all. Those who question the validity of Kuhn's model should feel themselves challenged to provide alternative interpretations of the genesis of revolutions in science. The present essay is intended less as a

critique of Kuhn's stimulating book than as a tentative formulation of some general ideas about the rise and development of concepts of organic evolution.

NOTES

1. Carl Linnaeus, *A General System of Nature . . . Translated from Gmelin's Last Edition . . .*, William Turton, trans. and ed. (London, 1806), 1:2; Georges Louis Leclerc, Comte de Buffon, *A Natural History, General and Particular . . .*, trans. William Smellie, 3rd ed. (London, 1791) 8:33–34.

2. Thomas S. Kuhn, "Energy Conservation as an Example of Simultaneous Discovery," in Marshall Clagett, ed., *Critical Problems in the History of Science* (Madison, Wisconsin, 1959), pp. 321–56.

3. John Ray, *The Wisdom of God Manifested in the Works of the Creation*, 3rd ed. (London, 1701), preface (not paged).

4. Thomas Jefferson, "A Memoir on the Discovery of Certain Bones of a Quadruped of the Clawed Kind in the Western Parts of Virginia," *Trans. Amer. Philos. Soc.* 4 (1799): 255–56.

5. George Bentham, "On the Recent Progress and Present State of Systematic Botany," *Report of the 11th Meeting of the British Association for the Advancement of Science in 1874* (London, 1875), 31 ff.

6. Étienne Geoffroy St. Hilaire, *Fragments biographies précédés d'études sur la vie, les ouvrages et la doctrine de BUFFON* (Paris, 1838), 3–157. In this essay Geoffroy St. Hilaire exhibits in a striking manner the contrast between the Linnaean-Cuvierian concept of natural history and that of Buffon and presents Lamarck's evolutionary philosophy and his own belief in the mutability of species as a continuation of Buffon's vision of nature as a system of *faits nécessaires*.

7. Bernard G. E. de la Ville sur Illon, Comte de Lacépède, *Histoire Naturelle des Poissons* (Paris, 1798–1804), 2:9–68.

8. The mental process by which Lamarck arrived at an evolutionary viewpoint in the last two or three years of the eighteenth century is difficult, if not impossible, to ascertain, but Lamarck's own statements lend considerable support to the interpretation I have advanced. In the opening sentences of the Appendix to his *Discours D'Ouverture de L'An X* he says:

> I thought for a long time that there were constant species in nature, and that they were constituted of the individuals belonging to each of them.

Now I am convinced that I was in error in this regard, and that there are really only individuals in nature.

The origin of this error, which I shared with many naturalists who still hold to it, is found in the *long duration* with respect to us of the same state of things in each place which each living body inhabits; but that duration of the same state of things for each place has a limit, and with plenty of time it undergoes mutations at each point of the surface of the globe which change the circumstances for all the living bodies inhabiting it. . . . Elevated places are constantly degraded, and everything which is detached is carried toward the low places. The beds of rivers, of streams, of seas even are insensibly displaced, as well as climates; in a word, everything on the surface of the earth changes little by little in situation, in form, in nature and aspect. . . . [Here he cites his *Hydrogéologie*]

Thus, Lamarck argues that the mutability of species follows from the mutability of the earth's surface and that both types of mutability are hidden from man by the extreme slowness of the changes that take place. In his *Discours D'Ouverture de L'An XI* (pp. 541–42) he makes it clear that organisms are *forced* to undergo change as a result of changes in their environments: ". . . we know . . . that a *forced and sustained change*, whether in the habits and manner of living of animals, or in the situation, the soil and the climate of plants, effects after a sufficient time a very remarkable mutation in the individuals exposed to it" (italics mine).

Finally, in his essay "Sur Les Fossiles" in his *Système Des Animaux Sans Vertèbres*, Lamarck reveals his awareness that, given the changes on the earth's surface postulated by geology, the alternative to transmutation of living forms is widespread extinction of species. Some naturalists, he says, have concluded from the lack of perfect resemblance between fossil and living species "that this globe has undergone a universal *bouleversement*, a general catastrophe, and that as a result a multitude of species of animals and of plants have been absolutely lost or destroyed." But Lamarck will have nothing to do with such a universal catastrophe, "which by its very nature regularizes nothing, confounds and disperses everything, and constitutes a very convenient means for naturalists who wish to explain everything and who do not take the trouble to observe and study the process which nature follows in regard to her productions and in everything which constitutes her domain." Instead, he undertakes to show "that although many of the fossil shells are different from all known marine shells, this by no means proves that the species of shells have been obliterated, but only that these species have changed in the course of time." ["Sur Les Fossiles," *Système Des Animaux Sans Vertèbres* (Paris, 1801), pp. 408–409. Translation mine.]

Thus, according to Lamarck, geology and paleontology present the naturalist with a choice: either (1) catastrophism and wholesale extinction of species, or (2) transmutationism on uniformitarian principles with little or no extinction of species. His own decision favors the second alternative, not only because of his uncompromising uniformitarianism in every branch of natural history but also because he finds in the transmutation hypothesis a neat solution to grave problems in taxonomy, an exhilarating sense of progress in nature, and a vindication of the wisdom of the Author of Nature, a wisdom that wholesale extinction of species would seem to impugn.

He seems never to have considered the possibility of combining uniformitarianism with acceptance of widespread extinction of species. It would take an Englishman to see the wise dispensation of the Creator in the competitive struggle for existence. [The passages from Lamarck's inaugural discourses are translated from the *Bulletin Scientifique de la France et de la Belgique*, vol. 40 (1906).]

9. This is not to say that there was no undermining of belief in the fixity of species among naturalists as the nineteenth century progressed. In botany Schleiden, Unger, and Rafinesque accepted transmutation by midcentury. But Darwin worked out his theory of natural selection in the thirties, largely in response to problems he had encountered on the voyage of the *Beagle*. Unfortunately, there has been too little research on the period 1830–1859 to warrant confident generalizations about the state of mind of naturalists in this period. My impression is that it would be difficult to prove the existence of a "crisis psychology" in the 1850s and impossible to do so for the 1830s.

10. John Playfair, *Illustrations of the Huttonian Theory of the Earth* (Edinburgh, 1802), pp. 469–70. I have used the facsimile reprint of this work (New York: Dover Publications, Inc., 1964). Playfair envisages the modification as well as the extinction of species driven into new habitats by man: ". . . the more innocent species fled to a distance from man, and being forced to retire into the most inaccessible parts, where their food was scanty, and their migration checked, they may have degenerated from the size and strength of their ancestors, and some species may have been entirely extinguished."

11. Charles Lyell, *Principles of Geology* . . . , 2nd ed. (London, 1832) 1:1.

12. Thomas Henry Huxley, "Evolution in Biology," *Darwiniana: Essays* (New York, 1908), p. 206. This essay was originally published in 1878.

13. Charles Darwin to the *Athenaeum*, Down, England, 5 May

1863, quoted in Francis Darwin, ed., *The Life and Letters of Charles Darwin* . . . (New York, 1898) 2:207.

SUGGESTED FURTHER READING

For commentaries on Thomas Kuhn's *The Structure of Scientific Revolutions* and Kuhn's replies to his critics, see Kuhn's "Postscript— 1969" to the second edition of that work (Chicago: University of Chicago Press, 1970), pp. 174–210; Kuhn's "Reflections on My Critics," in I. Lakatos and A. Musgrave, eds., *Criticism and the Growth of Knowledge* (Cambridge: Cambridge University Press, 1970), pp. 231–278; Kuhn's "Second Thoughts on Paradigms," in Frederick Suppe, ed., *The Structure of Scientific Theories*, 2nd ed. (Urbana: University of Illinois Press, 1974), pp. 459–482; and Gary Gutting, ed., *Paradigms and Revolutions: Criticisms and Applications of Thomas Kuhn's Philosophy of Science* (Notre Dame, Ind.: University of Notre Dame Press, 1980).

On the contrasting conceptions of natural history of Linnaeus and Buffon, see James L. Larson, *Reason and Experience: The Representation of Natural Order in the Work of Carl von Linné[3]* (Berkeley, Los Angeles, London: University of California Press, 1971); Frans A. Stafleu, *Linnaeus and the Linnaeans: The Spreading of Their Ideas in Systematic Botany, 1735–1789* (Utrecht: A. Oosthoek's Uitgeversmaatschappij, 1971); Philip R. Sloan, "The Buffon-Linnaeus Controversy," *Isis* 67 (1976): 356–357, and "Buffon, German Biology, and the Historical Interpretation of Biological Species," *British Journal of the History of Science* 12 (1979): 109–153.

On the ideas of Cuvier, Lamarck, and the Natur-philosophers, see William Coleman, *George Cuvier, Zoologist: A Study in the History of Evolution Theory* (Cambridge, Mass.: Harvard University Press, 1964); Richard W. Burkhardt, *The Spirit of System: Lamarck and Evolutionary Biology* (Cambridge, Mass.: Harvard University Press, 1977); Ernst Mayr, "Lamarck Revisited," *Journal of the History of Biology* 5 (1972): 55–94; M. J. S. Rudwick, *The Meaning of Fossils* (London: Macdonald, 1972); Peter J. Bowler, *Fossils and Progress: Paleontology and the Idea of Progressive Evolution in the Nineteenth Century* (New York: Science History Publications, 1967); Edward S. Russell, *Form and Function, A Contribution to the History of Animal Morphology* (London: John Murray, 1916).

On the general nature of the Darwinian revolution and its relation to earlier developments in natural history, see Ernst Mayr, "The Nature of the Darwinian Revolution," *Science* 176 (1972): 981–989;

Michael Ghiselin, *The Triumph of the Darwinian Method* (Berkeley and Los Angeles: University of California Press, 1969) and "The Individual in the Darwinian Revolution," *New Literary History* 3 (1979): 113–134; John C. Greene, *The Death of Adam: Evolution and Its Impact on Western Thought* (Ames: Iowa State University Press, 1959) and "Reflections on the Progress of Darwin Studies," *Journal of the History of Biology* 8 (1975): 243–273; Michael Ruse, *The Darwinian Revolution: Science Red in Tooth and Claw* (Chicago and London: University of Chicago Press, 1979); Howard E. Gruber and Paul H. Barrett, *Darwin on Man* (New York: E. P. Dutton, 1974); Dov Ospovat, *The Development of Darwin's Theory: Natural History, Natural Theology, and Natural Selection, 1838–1859*, forthcoming from the Cambridge University Press.

4

BIOLOGY AND SOCIAL THEORY IN THE NINETEENTH CENTURY: AUGUSTE COMTE AND HERBERT SPENCER

The simultaneous emergence of evolutionary theories in biology and sociology in the nineteenth century presents an interesting problem in historical interpretation. How were these two types of evolutionary theory related to each other? Was one derived from the other? Did they develop independently of each other? Was there a continuing interaction between the two? If so, what was the nature of the interaction? The present essay attempts to take a first step toward solving this problem by analyzing the relation of biological to sociological theory in the writings of Auguste Comte and Herbert Spencer.

The first truly evolutionary speculations in modern social theory appeared at approximately the same time as the first transformist ideas in biology. The same mid-eighteenth-century years that produced the speculations of Maupertuis and Diderot also produced Rousseau's *Discourse on the Origin and Foundations of Inequality Among Men*.[1] In this famous essay Rousseau developed a theory of human evolution in a purely speculative manner, by thinking away all of man's acquired characteristics so as to discover original human nature. He arrived at the conclusion that man had begun his career on earth as a brutelike creature distinguished from other animals only by his ability to perfect himself, that is, to invent ways and means of ameliorating his condition. Given this ability and the pressure of circumstances, the development of society, language, and the arts and sciences followed necessarily. Rousseau was uncertain whether to regard the progress of civilization as a blessing or a curse to mankind, but as the century wore on, developments in commerce and industry, combined with the revelations of geology, paleontology, and ethnology, produced a growing conviction that both nature and history were inherently progressive. Then came the French Revolution, posing its great question as to the future of Western civilization and awakening hope that reason might supplant custom as the molder of social institutions. On every hand there were proposals for creating a social science, a science that would reorder society, banish superstition, and guide mankind along the path of perpetual progress.

Nineteenth-century social science took its general character from these events and aspirations. It was highly normative in orientation, claiming to disclose man's duty and destiny as well as the solution of his immediate political and economic problems. Except for its "dismal" branch, political economy, it took progress for granted and set out to discover the laws of historical development. Theories of social evolution proliferated, as theories of the earth had in the eighteenth century. The striking resemblance between these two types of speculation was more than coincidental, for, given the conviction of gradual progress from a primitive condition whether of man or of the earth, the problem was to explain the assumed development by means of a few judiciously selected principles supported by an assortment of judiciously selected facts. In both cases attempts at scientific explanation ranged all the way from mere speculation to profound analysis based on careful investigation. A broad comparative study of these evolutionary theories would throw much light on the history of thought in the eighteenth and nineteenth centuries. The present paper, limited as it is to the social theories of Comte and Spencer, can do little more than suggest the possibilities inherent in this field of research.

The genesis of nineteenth-century social science is nowhere better illustrated than in the life and works of Auguste Comte, the founder of positivism. Born at Montpellier in 1798, he received an excellent training in the exact sciences at the École Polytechnique in Paris, where he soon distinguished himself by his mathematical talents and his republican fervor.

There followed several years of intensive study and political agitation, 1817–25, during which Comte collaborated with Count Henri de Saint-Simon in the latter's various literary projects, meanwhile developing his own ideas. These took definite shape in Comte's first and briefer *System of Positive Polity*, published under Saint-Simon's auspices in 1824. Saint-Simon died in the following year, and Comte soon after began a course of private lectures, the famous *Cours de philosophie positive*, which, published in six fat volumes between 1830 and 1842, laid the theoretical groundwork for his system of practical polity and established his claim to be one of the founders of the science that he named *sociology*.[2]

How did Comte arrive at his conception of sociology as a science concerned primarily with the laws of social evolution? In his earliest writings, dating from the period of his collaboration with Saint-Simon, Comte took as his starting point the moral and spiritual anarchy of post-Revolutionary Europe, an anarchy reflected in political instability, social unrest, and intellectual chaos. In Comte's opinion, the old order had been demolished, not by the French Revolution, but by the steady growth of science, undermining in its progress the system of beliefs and sentiments that held the aristocratic order together and gave it moral prestige. God was dead, and little could be done to restore social harmony and political stability until a new system of positive beliefs was erected on scientific foundations. "The period has . . . at last arrived," wrote Comte, "when the human mind, as the final result of all its previous labours, can complete the ensemble of Natural Philosophy by reducing Social phenomena, as all others have been reduced, to Positive theories. . . . Such is the great philosophic effort reserved for the Nineteenth Century by the natural progress of our intellectual development."[3]

As he set himself to this task, Comte examined one by one the efforts that had already been made toward constituting a science of society. First, there were those like Condorcet who held out the hope that mathematics, especially the calculus of probabilities, could be applied to the analysis of human behavior. But Comte, mathematician though he was, regarded this as a false lead. He was convinced that the phenomena of life and of society were too complex for mathematical treatment. Secondly, there were the political economists, the champions and analysts of the new commercial and industrial order, who claimed to have demonstrated the self-regulating character of the economy and thereby to have established a scientific basis for a policy of *laissez faire*. But, although Comte had great respect for Adam Smith and Jean Baptiste Say, he found their conception of social science too narrow for his purposes. They explained everything in terms of the rational pursuit of self-interest, assuming a kind of preordained harmony between individual interests and the welfare of society. It was simply not true, said Comte, that men acted only, or even mainly, from calculation or that they were capable of calculating wisely when they did. Doubtless there was a tendency toward equilibrium in economic affairs, but this equilibrium was by no means automatic, and it presupposed a moral order capable of moderating class antagonisms and international rivalries and of mitigating the divisive effects of the ever-increasing division of labor. Political economy was at best a partial and one-sided social science, incapable of creating or sustaining the moral order that it presupposed or of providing an adequate basis for scientific prevision.[4]

Finally, there were the bio-sociologists, men like George Cabanis, Antoine Destutt de Tracy, and Francis Joseph Gall, who envisaged the new social science as a branch of zoology. In Comte's opinion, however, these writers overlooked the crucial characteristic of human society: "the progressive influence of the successive generations upon each other." Biology, he declared, was relevant only insofar as it disclosed man's natural endowment and insofar as it could "throw light on the formation of primitive aggregations of men, and deduce the history of the childhood of our race down to the period when the first impulse of Civilisation was given by the creation of Language."[5] From that point on, it was the province of social physics to discover "by what necessary chain of successive transformations the human race, starting from a condition barely superior to that of a society of great apes, has been gradually led up to the present stage of

European civilisation."[6] Thus, social physics was the study of the progress of civilization. That civilization had progressed seemed to Comte too obvious to require proof. Its progress was to be seen in the course of human history as a whole and in the recurrence of an identical pattern of historical development in civilizations isolated from each other. The recurrence of this pattern seemed to prove beyond doubt that social evolution was not haphazard but issued inevitably from "the fundamental laws of human organization" and was governed by "a natural law of progress, independent of all combinations, and dominating them."[7]

What were the sources of this evolutionary conception, embodied in Comte's famous law of the three successive stages of civilization: the theological, the metaphysical, and the positive? It was not from biology that his inspiration was drawn; his writings and letters in the formative period sing the praises of Bichat and Gall but not of Lamarck. His intellectual debt in social theory lay in a different direction: to Condorcet's *Sketch of an Historical Picture of the Progress of the Human Mind*, to the historical writings of Hume and Robertson, and to the ideas of Saint-Simon. Above all, his doctrine emerged from his studies in the history and philosophy of science, studies begun at the École Polytechnique and subsequently broadened to include the life sciences. The history of science and technology was the example *par excellence* of cumulative growth, of the progressive transformation of society by the progressive development of positive knowledge. It seemed to show that each of the sciences had passed through a theological and a metaphysical stage before becoming truly scientific, and the philosophy of science established the necessary sequence in which the various sciences underwent this transformation. Thus, the growth of science and the scientific attitude indicated the general direction of historical development, and the discovery of the preordained sequence in which the sciences attained a positive status made it possible to locate Comte's own age in the stream of history and to predict the outcome of the entire development. For the science of society was in its very nature a science of the whole historical sequence. With the establishment of sociology, all fields of thought would have become positive in orientation, and historical development would have reached its final phase. Emancipated from theological and metaphysical conceptions, civilized by the growth of science and industry, unified by a common allegiance to science and the scientific method, men would abandon their attempts to control each other and would unite in efforts to increase human happiness by controlling nature.[8]

Comte's biological philosophy is set forth in the third volume of his *Cours de philosophie positive*, his sociology in the three following volumes. It will be interesting to treat the two together in order to discover how they were related to each other. As has been indicated, Comte's social evolutionism was not derived from his biological studies. He specifically rejected Lamarck's development hypothesis, but not because it implied the transmissibility of acquired characters. Comte regarded it as an "incontestable principle" that there was a tendency "to fix in races, by hereditary transmission . . . modifications at first direct and individual, so as to augment them gradually in each generation if the action of the environment continues unaltered."[9] Lamarck's error, he maintained, lay in assuming that nature had unlimited time at her disposal and that organisms were indefinitely modifiable. The assumption of unlimited time he considered a defect "so glaring that there is no need to examine it specially." The indefinite mutability of species, on the other hand, had been disproved by the "luminous argumentation" of Cuvier. The species observed by Aristotle had not changed since his day, the Egyptian mummies exhibited a physical type still preserved among their descendants, and the fossil record provided numerous examples of species that had remained unaltered throughout geologic time. Plants and animals that had been domesticated and transported to new environments had not been transmuted into new species. The same was true of the human species despite the variety of climates to which it had been exposed. Finally, the cases were legion in which organisms had failed to adapt themselves to changed circumstances. Many mammals had been rendered extinct by the spread of human civilization, and some primitive races of men had all but disappeared from the earth. Extinction, not progressive modification, was the consequence of alterations that destroyed the equilibrium between organism and environment. "If," said Comte, "one conceives that all possible organisms were successively placed during a suitable time in all imaginable environments, most of these organisms would necessarily end by disappearing, thus leaving alive only those that could satisfy the general laws of that fundamental equilibrium: it is probably through a succession of analogous eliminations that the biological harmony was established little by little on our planet, where indeed we still see it modifying itself unceasingly in a similar manner."[10] Thus, Comte invoked the principle of the survival of the fit to account for the gradual establishment of the present equilibrium of life and its terrestrial environment, but he made no provision for the emergence of new species to take the place of those extinguished in the course of time. Only his limited time scheme prevented this omission from becoming a serious embarrassment. If he had thought the matter through, he would have had to admit either the idea of special creations, a conception totally inconsistent with his positivistic outlook, or some kind of development hypothesis, unless he was willing to envisage the progressive extinction of all forms of life.

The inadequacy of Comte's discussion of the development hypothesis is explained in large measure by his rather restricted view of the field of biology. His main interest was in anatomy and physiology, which comprised for him *la biologie proprement dite*. Natural history in Buffon's broad sense he recognized only as a "concrete, particular, and hence secondary science" subordinate to the more abstract, general, and basic disciplines of pure biology. Geology and paleontology, with their strong historical orientation, scarcely entered into his calculations. In Comte's view, biology began by assuming a certain equilibrium between the organism and its environment and then sought to discover the laws of their interaction: "in a word, to connect constantly, in a manner both general and special, the twofold idea of organ and of milieu by a means of the idea of function."[11] Viewed statically, this was a problem in comparative anatomy; viewed dynamically, it was a problem in physiology. Comparative anatomy, grounding itself in Bichat's work on the tissues of the body, aimed first of all at deriving all the various elementary tissues from a single primitive tissue: "the essential term of every organism."[12] Moreover, it moved toward a natural classification of living forms, assigning each its distinctive place in the organic hierarchy, which Comte conceived as descending from the adult male human being as the primordial and most perfect type to the lowest of the low in the vegetable kingdom. It was in this connection, in showing how the concept of the scale of nature would assist in perfecting the natural system of classification, that Comte felt called upon to discuss Lamarck's development hypothesis, which, though it did not impugn the basic conception of the scale of being, placed enormous difficulties in the way of assigning species and genera their proper places in that scale. Lamarck's hypothesis disposed of, Comte found it possible to "regard as demonstrated the necessary discontinuity of the great biological series." "The various transitions," he conceded, "can, doubtless, eventually become more gradual either by the discovery of intermediate organisms or by a more careful study of those already known. But the essential fixity of the species guarantees that the series will always be composed of terms clearly distinct, separated by unbreakable intervals."[13]

Although Comte did not believe in organic evolution, biology and biological analogy played a large role in his social theory. In the first place, he drew from biology, especially from the writings of Gall, his theory of basic human nature, that nature that made possible and inevitable man's social evolution, determined its general direction of movement, and prescribed the limits of its variability. According to Comte, Gall had demonstrated scientifically the preponderance of the affective over the intellectual side of human nature and had proved the innate sociability of man, "in virtue of an instinctive tendency toward common life independently of all personal calculation and often contrary to the most energetic individual interests."[14] Without this preponderance of the emotions, without this natural sociability, the formation of society would have been impossible, the sentiments being necessary to stimulate intellectual activity and to give it a definite goal, as well as to restrain man's egotistic impulses in behalf of social order. On this "double opposition" of man's affective and intellectual nature and his social and egotistic impulses society was founded. These propositions Comte believed had been given a firm scientific basis by the phrenological researches of Franz Joseph Gall.

Comte also drew from biology his distinction between the statical and the dynamical approach to the study of organisms. Social statics he defined as "the fundamental study of the conditions of existence of society."[15] Every system, he declared, requires and presupposes a certain solidarity or internal harmony, the subjection of the parts to the functioning of the whole. In biological organisms the activities of the various tissues and organs are coordinated more or less automatically by means of the nervous system. In human society the coordination of actions is rooted in the sentiments and is moral in character. Its nonintellectual, predominantly affective, character is best exemplified in the basic social unit, which is not the individual but the family. In the family is to be found the primitive division of labor, based on differences of sex and age. In the family is to be found that social solidarity, that *union véritable*, which is "essentially moral and very incidentally intellectual,"* and which is "destined to satisfy directly the ensemble of our sympathetic instincts independently of any thought of active and continued cooperation toward any end whatever."[16] In the later stages of social evolution, Comte conceded, voluntary cooperation based on rational appreciation of self-interest plays a larger and larger role in social coordination, but even then social solidarity is predominantly affective in character. Voluntary cooperation, far from having given birth to society, presupposes it. As the division of labor progresses, the moral ties uniting society are loosened, and increased social control is required to supply the deficiencies of the ever-less-automatic social harmony. Thus, a true social science, far from assuming the natural identity of interests in modern society, perceives the tendency of industrial evolution to dissolve the bonds of social solidarity in the acid of self-interest and class interest and moves to prescribe the necessary social remedies, warned by its knowledge of social statics that the elements of the social organism cannot safely be viewed in abstraction from the functioning of the whole.[17]

So much for Comte's social statics, notable for its discussion of the basis of social order, or what, by analogy to biology, might be called the internal conditions of existence of the social organism. One might suppose that Comte would carry the analogy farther and consider the external conditions of existence of particular societies, exhibiting the functions of the various social organs and their modifications in response to changes in the environment, as Spencer was later to do. Such was not the case, however. For Comte was less interested in the evolution of particular societies than in the progress of the human race, more especially the white race. The pecularity of human society, he insisted, lay in the influence of each generation on succeeding generations, a peculiarity that tended more and more "to transform artificially the species into a single individual, immense and eternal, endowed with a constantly progressive action on exterior nature."[18] Through the cumulative developments in each particular society and the ever-increasing contact and borrowing among different societies there was set in motion an irreversible development of the human race as a whole, a development that could terminate only in the universal brotherhood of man. The direction and general character of this historical process was dictated by man's biological endowment, his original complement of abilities, instincts, and impulses. Social evolution could not alter basic human nature, but it could and did alter the relative influence of its various components, gradually bringing about the ascendancy of the social, peaceable, and intellectual side of man's nature over the egotistic, combative, and sensual side. In this respect, said Comte, it was necessary to invoke the "undeniable principle of the illustrious Lamarck" concerning "the necessary influence of a homogeneous and continued exercise in producing, in every animal organism, and especially in man, an improvement susceptible of being gradually fixed in the race after a persistence sufficiently prolonged."[19]

The evolution of humanity was best observed, however, in its intellectual development, especially in the development of science and the scientific spirit, which, though intimately connected with social and economic changes, was nevertheless the prime mover in history. To grasp the laws of this development it was necessary to apply the comparative method historically, exhibiting the progressive complication of social organization and cultural interdependence in the progress of mankind. Thus, whereas in biology progressive gradation was conceived as being given once and for all in the organic hierarchy or great chain of being, in sociology it was regarded as evolved in the course of time, as moving gradually toward full realization. And just as in biology the progressive gradation of the organic hierarchy was thought to be recapitulated in the embryological development of the individual human organism, so the *échelle sociale*, or progressive societal development, was conceived as mirrored in the mental life history of each individual in civilized society.[20]

The cause of human progress Comte found in the very nature of man. It was implicit in "that fundamental instinct, a complex resultant of the combination of all our natural tendencies, which directly pushes man to ameliorate his condition incessantly in every way . . . to develop always in every regard the whole of his physical, moral, and intellectual life as much as the circumstances in which he is placed permit."[21] Thus, for Comte, circumstances were not so much the cause as the occasion of human development. Climate, geography, racial mixture, social conditions, political policies, and the like might accelerate or retard it, but they could never alter its direction or halt its onward progress. For in every situation, favorable or unfavorable, men would seek to understand their world and control it, and so seeking they would be led by slow but inevitable steps from a theological to a metaphysical to a scientific way of thinking and from a militaristic and predatory to an industrial and peaceful way of living, a transition necessarily accompanied by a corresponding development of the higher brain centers. It was in this "exact harmony" between the findings of historical analysis and the expectations derived from the biological theory of human nature that sociological science found its ultimate verification.

Herbert Spencer provides an interesting contrast to Auguste Comte. Like Comte, Spencer ranged the whole gamut of the sciences and sought to bring human nature and society within the scope of scientific method. Like Comte, he rejected supernaturalism and the search for ultimate reality, confining himself to investigating the laws governing phenomena. Like Comte, he believed that social science, since it aimed at discovering the laws of historical development, held the key to man's duty and destiny and afforded a scientific basis for individual ethics and social policy. But whereas Comte rejected the competitive society of the nineteenth century as anarchic in both theory and practice, regarding it as a mere transition between the community of the medieval period and the coming community of the scientific age, Spencer glorified the individualism of his day and modeled his society of the future on its pattern. Far from rejecting the social atomism of the eighteenth century, Spencer sought to ground it firmly in the science of life and in a general view of the cosmos. Whereas for Comte progressive development was the peculiar characteristic of human society, for Spencer it was the general attribute of existence, the universal law of nature. In Comte's view biology was relevant to social theory chiefly as it threw light on man's original nature; in Spencer's it provided a model of social theory in both its statical and its dynamical aspects.

In its earliest manifestations Spencer's thought exhibited two features that were to characterize it to the end: (1) a firm belief in the laissez-faire policy in social and political matters, and (2) adherence to the development hypothesis. It was about 1840 that Spencer first read Lyell's *Principles of Geology*. The arguments there advanced against Lamarck's zoological philosophy, far from inducing Spencer to reject it, inclined him to accept it. "Its congruity with the course of procedure throughout things at large, gave it an irresistible attraction," Spencer wrote later, "and my belief in it never afterwards wavered, much as I was, in after years, ridiculed for entertaining it."[22] No less ardent was his attachment to the laissez-faire principles of classical political economy. His first book, *Social Statics*, published in 1850, attempted to strengthen those principles by deriving them from a broader social science rooted in an evolutionary conception of nature, human nature, and society. The strongly normative character of the inquiry was indicated by the author's definitions of social statics and social dynamics. Social statics, Spencer declared, concerns itself with "the equilibrium of a perfect society." "It seeks to determine what laws we must obey for the obtainment of complete happiness."[23] Social dynamics, by contrast, studies "the forces by which society is advanced toward perfection," that is, the influences that gradually dispose human beings to obey the laws conditioning their happiness. The perfect society is one in which every individual is free to exercise his natural faculties to the limit and in which individuals have lost all inclination to engage in activities harmful to others.

By defining social statics as the study of the conditions of equilibrium in a *perfect* society, Spencer introduced a dynamic point of view immediately. Obviously the society of his own day was not the perfect society; it did not give each individual equal freedom to exercise his faculties, nor was it composed of individuals whose desires were completely compatible with the rights of others. These imperfections in European society were explained, said Spencer, by the fact that human nature had not yet become adapted to the conditions of life in the modern industrial order. All imperfection consisting in "unfitness to the conditions of existence," this unfitness must consist "in having a faculty or faculties in excess; or in having a faculty or faculties deficient; or in both."[24] In what respect, then, was modern man maladapted to the conditions of modern life? In the sense, answered Spencer, that his original nature was adapted to a primitive condition of life, a condition in which survival depended on a fierce struggle with nature and with other men, for

the aboriginal man must have a constitution adapted to the work he has to perform, joined with a dormant capability of developing into the ultimate man when the conditions of existence permit. To the end that he may prepare the earth for its future inhabitants . . . he must possess a character fitting him to clear it of races endangering his life, and races occupying the space required by mankind. . . . In other words, he must be what we call a savage, and must be left to acquire fitness for social life as fast as the conquest of the earth renders social life possible.[25]

Thus, man began as a brutelike creature hard pressed to survive. The pressure of necessity drove him into the social state and led him to invent techniques whereby the circumstances of life were ameliorated. Man's inventiveness transformed the conditions of his existence, and the new conditions of existence operated in turn to transform human nature. In primitive society, men could be held together only by the crude forces of fear and hero worship. But as civilization progressed, the moral sense, based on sympathy and the instinct of personal rights, grew in strength, and voluntary cooperation began to supplant coercive arrangements. When fully developed, the moral sense would render government both unnecessary and impossible. This whole progress of events was predetermined from the beginning:

> given an unsubdued earth; given the being man, appointed to overspread and occupy it; given the laws of life what they are; and no other series of changes than that which has taken place, could have taken place. . . . Progress, therefore, is not an accident, but a necessity. Instead of civilization being artificial, it is a part of nature; all of a piece with the development of the embryo or the unfolding of a flower. The modifications mankind have undergone, and are still undergoing, result from a law underlying the whole organic creation; and provided the human race continues, and the constitution of things remains the same, those modifications must end in completeness.[26]

They were, Spencer declared, intended to do so by the Creator, who had implanted in man "desires for improvement, and aspirations after perfection, ultimately tending to produce a higher moral and intellectual condition of the world."

Given the fact and the general pattern of societal development, what were the implications for social policy? Like Comte, Spencer maintained that social policy, though it might accelerate or retard the predetermined course of social evolution, could never halt it or deflect it from its main line of march. But whereas Comte envisaged an ever-increasing interposition of social control to make up for the gradual dissolution of social solidarity, Spencer anticipated the gradual withering away of government as the individuals composing society acquired the natures requisite for the successful operation of a free society. This process of adaptation could best be hastened, he thought, by throwing the individual ever more on his own, thus compelling him to develop industry, thrift, foresight, moral independence, and capacity for voluntary cooperation. "It is not by humanly-devised agencies, good as these may be in their way," he declared, "but it is by the never-ceasing action of circumstances upon men—by the constant pressure of their new conditions upon them—that the required change is mainly effected."[27] This action, he asserted, is akin to "the stern discipline of Nature" in the biological realm. Just as in nature the struggle for existence operates to remove the sickly, the malformed, the unfit, so in society competition eliminates the ignorant, the improvident, and the lazy. "Partly by weeding out those of lowest development, and partly by subjecting those who remain to the never-ceasing discipline of experience, nature secures the growth of a race who shall both understand the conditions of existence, and be able to act up to them. It is impossible in any degree to suspend this discipline by stepping in between ignorance and its consequences, without, to a corresponding degree, suspending progress."[28] Such an intervention, moreover, would interfere with the automatic processes of internal adjustment whereby the energies of the social organism are directed where they are most needed.

Despite its title, *Social Statics* was concerned more with the progress than with the structure of society. Spencer's treatment of social structure and of the basis of social order was very sketchy; it appealed to physical and chemical rather than to biological analogies. Society was conceived as an aggregate of individuals, and the proposition was advanced that the characters of the individuals comprising the social aggregate determine the nature of the aggregate. Stability in the social system was conceived to arise from the properties of the constituent units. "Sympathy and the instinct of rights," Spencer wrote,

> do not always coexist in equal strength any more than other faculties do. Either of them may be present in normal amount, whilst the other is almost wanting. . . . The instinct of rights, being of itself entirely selfish, merely impels its possessor to maintain his own privileges. Only by the sympathetic excitement of it, is a desire to behave equitably to others awakened; and when sympathy is absent such a desire is impossible. Nevertheless this does not affect the general proposition, that where there exists the usual amount of sympathy, respect for the rights of others will be great or small, according as the amount of the instinct of personal rights is great or small.[29]

Thus, "the first principle of a code for the right ruling of humanity in its state of *multitude,* is to be found in humanity in its state of *unitude*— . . . the moral forces upon which social equilibrium depends, are resident in the social atom— man; and . . , if we would understand the nature of those forces, and the laws of that equilibrium, we must look for them in the human constitution."[30]

Spencer's treatment of social dynamics also left a good deal to be desired. He asserted again and again that the historical change in the circumstances of man's existence had produced and continued to produce a change in the characters of the individuals composing society. But as to what had brought about the change of circumstances he had little to say, except for the suggestion that a change in character, once accomplished, operated to produce new changes in circumstances. The reason for Spencer's vagueness on this point is not hard to guess. The question of the causes underlying these changes was an historical one, and Spencer was not interested in history.

> You can draw no inference from the facts and alleged facts of history [he wrote his friend Edward Lott] without your concep-

tions of human nature entering into that inference: and unless your conceptions of human nature are true your inference will be vicious. But if your conceptions of human nature be true you need none of the inferences drawn from history for your guidance. If you ask how is one to get a true theory of humanity, I reply—study it in the facts you see around you and in the general laws of life. For myself, looking as I do at humanity as the highest result yet of the evolution of life on the earth, I prefer to take in the whole series of phenomena from the beginning as far as they are ascertainable. I, too, am a lover of history; but it is the history of the Cosmos as a whole.[31]

In view of this statement, it is not surprising that when Spencer did hazard a speculation concerning the causes of historical change, it was quasi-biological in character. In his "Theory of Population," published in 1852, he found the "proximate cause of progress" in the pressure of population on resources. Starting from two propositions: (1) that the power of self-preservation varies inversely as the power of reproduction, and (2) that the degree of fertility varies inversely as the development of the nervous system, he endeavored to show that population pressure in any species would operate to produce complication of the nervous system and a decline in fertility, thus reestablishing an equilibrium between population and the means of subsistence. Since the human race was rapidly multiplying in numbers, it followed on this hypothesis that mankind must also be undergoing a development in nervous organization that must eventually diminish the supply of vital energy available for the reproduction of the species. That such a development was actually taking place was apparent, said Spencer, from the difference in cranial capacity between the savages of Australia and Africa and the civilized peoples of Europe, a difference of 30 percent from lowest to highest. The reasons for the development were equally apparent, for

this inevitable redundancy of numbers—this constant increase of people beyond the means of subsistence—involving as it does an increasing stimulus to better the modes of producing food and other necessaries—involves also an increasing demand for skill, intelligence, and self-control—involves, therefore, a constant exercise of these, that is—involves a gradual growth of them. Every improvement is at once the product of a higher form of humanity, and demands that higher form of humanity to carry it into practice.[32]

It should not be thought, Spencer warned, that every people hard pressed to subsist inevitably undergo a progressive improvement in character. Although all mankind are subjected sooner or later to nature's stern discipline, not all peoples benefit by it. "For, necessarily, families and races whom this increasing difficulty of getting a living which excess of fertility entails, does not stimulate to improvements in production—that is, to greater mental activity—are on the high road to extinction; and must ultimately be supplanted by those whom the pressure does so stimulate."[33] Those who survive the ordeal, whether as individuals or as races, are nature's elect, and their survival insures the onward progress of mankind and the decrease in human fertility required to adjust population to resources. Thus, population pressure is the great engine of progress whether in nature or in society.

It produced the original diffusion of the race. It compelled men to abandon predatory habits and take to agriculture. It led to the clearing of the earth's surface. It forced men into the social state; made social organization inevitable; and has developed the social sentiments. It has stimulated to progressive improvements in production, and to increased skill and intelligence. It is daily pressing us into closer contact and more mutually-dependent relationships. And after having caused, as it ultimately must, the due peopling of the globe, and the bringing of all its habitable parts into the highest state of culture—after having brought all processes for the satisfaction of human wants to the greatest perfection—after having, at the same time, developed the intellect into complete competency for its work, and the feelings into complete fitness for social life—after having done all this, we see that the pressure of population, as it gradually finishes its work, must gradually bring itself to an end.[34]

As the decade of the fifties progressed, Spencer applied the development hypothesis to an ever-widening range of phenomena. In his *Principles of Psychology*, first published in 1855, he endeavored to establish psychology as a branch of evolutionary biology by showing that mental processes, like physiological processes, are modes of adaptation of the organism to its environment and that in both cases nature displays a "progressive evolution of the correspondence between organism and environment." Having established the general similarity of mental processes and life processes in general, Spencer proceeded to trace the various gradations of these modes of awareness of the environment from the simplest organic responses to environmental stimuli to the highest thought processes of human beings, exhibiting the progressive extension of the correspondence of internal and external relations in space and time and in generality and speciality, and indicating the necessary connection between this progressive correspondence and the progressive complication in organic structure, particularly in the nervous system. At this point in the argument, Spencer tacitly introduced the development hypothesis, arguing that the progressive complication in nervous organization and in the accompanying correspondences of internal and external conditions had slowly evolved in response to changes in the environment. On this assumption he was able to show that not only reflex and instinctive sequences but also the very forms of thought, the Kantian categories, were products of mental evolution.

> The doctrine that the connections among our ideas are determined by experience [he wrote] must, in consistency, be extended not only to all the connections established by the accumulated experiences of every individual, but to all those established by the accumulated experiences of every race. The abstract law of Intelligence being, that the strength of the tendency which the antecedent of any psychical change has to be followed by its consequent, is proportionate to the persistency of the union between the external things they symbolize; it becomes the resulting law of all concrete intelligences, that the strength of the tendency for such consequent to follow its antecedent, is, other things being equal, proportionate to the number of times it has thus followed in experience. The harmony of the inner tendencies and the outer persistencies, is, in all its complications, explicable on the single principle that the outer persistencies produce the inner tendencies.[35]

Thus, associations of ideas may be inherited.

Throughout the course of this argument Spencer appealed frequently to the facts or alleged facts of human history in support of his contentions. On the one hand, he cited the progress of science and technology as evidence of the ever-widening correspondence between man and his environment. On the other hand, he viewed the progress of humanity in general as a product of gradual biological improvement in the human stock, involving the superseding and displacement of inferior varieties of human beings by superior types, these superior types being evolved in response to the more complicated physiographical and social environments in which some races of men found themselves. In Spencer's mind the difference between the "small-brained savage" and the "large-brained European" was the strongest kind of evidence favoring the hypothesis that both brain structure and mental processes were the cumulative product of the life habits of the race, life habits dictated primarily by the conditions of existence.

> We know [he declared] that there are warlike, peaceful, nomadic, maritime, hunting, commercial races—races that are independent or slavish, active or slothful—races that display great varieties of disposition; we know that many of these, if not all, have a common origin; and hence there can be no question that these varieties of disposition, which have a more or less evident relation to habits of life, have been gradually induced and established in successive generations, and have become organic.[36]

The logical implication of Spencer's argument was that the progress of humanity had been accomplished by a competition of races in which superior types produced by more favorable combinations of circumstances had pushed aside those types whose life circumstances had been less conducive to mental growth.

Spencer produced no general work on sociology in this period, but the trend of his thought concerning society was made clear in a series of essays bearing such titles as "The Genesis of Science," "Manners and Fashions," "The Social Organism," "Overlegislation," and the like.[37] In general, the themes of these essays were those of his earlier writings. There was a firm insistence on the genetic approach to the study of social institutions. Society was again compared to a biological organism, and the comparison was worked out in greater detail. Social institutions were held to develop "under the pressure of wants and necessities," their particular forms being dictated by the characters of the peoples involved, these characters, in turn, being the cumulative and slowly changing product of varying life circumstances. The poles of this evolutionary process were primitive society, represented by the "almost structureless" aggregations of Australian savages, and the highly complex and interdependent society of Europe. The sequence of institutional development was viewed as dictated by the relative importance of the various kinds of social institutions for the survival of the race. First came arrangements for defense, then political institutions, then economic organization and the division of labor, then science, literature, and the arts, each undergoing a progressive complication in its turn. This institutional growth was conceived as self-regulating and beneficent so long as it continued unhampered by well-intended but ill-conceived government regulation.

There was little new in all of this. The main novelty of these years, apart from Spencer's venture into psychology, was his steady progress toward a philosophical synthesis in which the concept of evolution played the central role. As Spencer himself pointed out, the time was ripe for a philosophical reconstruction that would tie together with a few leading concepts and broad generalizations the growing accumulation of empirical knowledge in the various fields of scientific inquiry. In his essay entitled "Progress: Its Law and Cause," published in 1857, he called attention to the fact that developmental concepts had invaded many fields of science, especially anatomy and physiology, but also geology, paleontology, astronomy, linguistics, and social theory. It was in the social sphere that he found his most conclusive evidence of the universal tendency toward progress. The nebular hypothesis had not yet been accepted by astronomers, and although Von Baer's researches in embryology had introduced developmental conceptions into anatomy and physiology, the evidence for and against a general evolution of organic forms was too evenly balanced to permit a clear conclusion. In human history, however, Spencer found overwhelming evidence of a progressive trend from homogeneity to heterogeneity. It was to be seen, he declared, in the multiplication of human races, in the transition from the relatively undeveloped brain of the barbarian to the superior mental capacity of the civilized European, in the growing complexity of political, social, and economic institutions, in the evolution of languages, in the growth of science, in every field of human endeavor. Progress was written into the constitution of the universe. It was "not an accident, not a thing within human control, but a beneficent necessity."[38]

A decade and a half of public discussion of Darwin's theory of evolution intervened between the publication of Spencer's essay on the law and cause of progress and the appearance of his major sociological treatises: *The Study of Sociology, Descriptive Sociology,* and *Principles of Sociology.* On the surface it seemed that his general point of view had changed but little. The description of the task of sociological science in *The Study of Sociology* had a familiar ring:

> Setting out, then, with this general principle, that the properties of its members determine the properties of the mass, we conclude that there must be a Social Science expressing the relations between the two. Beginning with types of men who form but small and incoherent social aggregates, such a science has to show in what way the individual qualities, intellectual and emotional, negative further aggregation. It has to explain how modifications of the individual nature, arising under modified conditions of life, make larger aggregates possible. It has to trace, in societies of some size, the genesis of the social relations, regulative and operative, into which the members fall. It has to exhibit the stronger and more prolonged influences which, by further modifying the characters of citizens, facilitate wider and closer unions with consequent further complexities of structure. . . . In every case its object is to interpret the growth, development, structure, and functions, of the social aggregate, as brought about by the mutual actions of individuals whose

natures are partly like those of all men, partly like those of kindred races, partly distinctive.

These phenomena have, of course, to be explained with due reference to the conditions each society is placed in—the conditions furnished by its locality and by its relation to neighboring societies. Noting this merely to prevent misapprehensions, the general fact which here concerns us, is that, given men having certain properties, an aggregate of such men must have certain derivative properties which form the subject-matter of a science.[39]

In the working out of these general principles, however, there were significant changes. The old polarity between primitive society, held together by force and fear, and modern society, based increasingly on voluntary cooperation, was now elaborated in a correlative distinction between militant and industrial societies, the former characterized by compulsory cooperation and centralized regulatory systems, the latter by voluntary cooperation, free exchange, and the diminution of centralized controls. Spencer was no longer certain, however, that the trend from the militant to the industrial type of society was inevitable and irreversible. He listed a whole series of factors that tended to delay and disfigure the transition and conceded the possibility that a society of the industrial type might regress to militancy "if international conflicts recur."[40] Indeed, he saw that very process of reversion taking place before his eyes in Western Europe.

This recognition of the contemporary regression to militancy and centralized controls was but one manifestation of a fundamental reorientation in Spencer's thinking about evolution. In his essay entitled "Progress: Its Law and Cause" Spencer had tended to identify change with development, that is, to think of change as developmental in its very nature, progress from homogeneity to heterogeneity following ineluctably from a basic law of change, namely, that "every active force produces more than one change." In social matters this progress was conceived as characterizing the development of each particular society as well as the development of humanity at large.[41] By the time of the sociological treatises, however, Spencer was less inclined to identify change and progress.

> Evolution [he wrote] is commonly conceived to imply in every-thing an intrinsic tendency to become something higher; but this is an erroneous conception of it. In all cases it is determined by the co-operation of inner and outer factors. This co-operation works changes until there is reached an equilibrium between the environing actions and the actions which the aggregate opposes to them—a complete equilibrium if the aggregate is without life, a moving equilibrium if the aggregate is living. Thereupon evolu-tion, continuing to show itself only in the progressing integration that ends in rigidity, practically ceases. If in the case of the living aggregates forming a species, the environing actions remain constant from generation to generation, the species remains constant. If the environing actions change, the species changes until it re-equilibrates itself with them. But it by no means follows that this change in the species constitutes a step in evolu-tion. Usually neither advance nor recession results; and often, certain previously-acquired structures being rendered super-fluous, there results a simpler form. Only now and then does the environing change initiate in the organism a new complication, and so produce a somewhat higher type. Hence the truth that while for immeasurable periods some types have neither ad-vanced nor receded, and while in other types there has been further evolution, there are many types in which retrogression has happened.

As with organic evolution, so with super-organic evolution. Though, taking the entire assemblage of societies, evolution may be held inevitable as an ultimate effect of the co-operating factors, intrinsic and extrinsic, acting on them all through indefi-nite periods of time; yet it cannot be held inevitable in each particular society, or even probable. A social organism, like an individual organism, undergoes modifications until it comes into equilibrium with environing conditions; and thereupon con-tinues without further change of structure. When the conditions are changed meteorologically, or geologically, or by alterations in the Flora and Fauna, or by migration consequent on pressure of population, or by flight before usurping races, some change of social structure is entailed. But this change does not necessarily imply advance. Often it is towards neither a higher nor a lower structure. Where the habitat entails modes of life that are inferior, some degradation results. Only occasionally is the new combination of factors such as to cause a change constituting a step in social evolution, and initiating a social type which spreads and supplants inferior social types. For with these super-organic aggregates, as with the organic aggregates, progression in some produces retrogression in others: the more-evolved societies drive the less-evolved societies into unfavourable habitats; and so entail on them decrease of size, or decay of structure.[42]

This revised version of evolution afforded a convenient explanation of the failure of some organisms, whether biological or social, to progress. It explained the anomalous fact that the Australian savages, notwithstanding their primitive social condition, had a complicated kinship structure and system of marriage rules—presumably a holdover from a higher stage from which they had regressed. In other respects, however, the new point of view had disturbing implications. It envisaged the progress of humanity as the outcome of race conflict, the progress being made by those races that happened to develop in such a way that they were able to "spread and supplant inferior social types." Such, according to Spencer, had been the history of human progress "throughout long periods," a history marked by "a continuous overrunning of the less powerful or less adapted by the more powerful or more adapted, a driving of inferior varieties into undesirable habitats, and, occasionally, an extermination of inferior varieties."[43] But if progress had occurred in this way in the past, why should it not be generated in the same way in the future? And if the militant, highly centralized form of society was better adapted to survival in the competition of races, what reason was there to regard the peaceable, industrial type as somehow higher or more evolved? Was not survival in the competitive conflict the test of superiority?

Spencer seems not to have grasped the full implication of his revised view of evolution. Having admitted that progress is neither necessary nor probable in any particular society, he nevertheless continued to invoke the analogy of the individual life cycle in opposing programs of radical social change, arguing that such programs served to retard "the normal course of evolution" in societies that adopted them. [44] Again, in his reply to James Martineau's attack on Darwinian evolution he argued that survival of the fittest was not necessarily or even probably survival of the best, [45] ignoring the fact that he had represented and continued to represent social progress as a product of race warfare in which "superior races" supplanted and even exterminated "inferior races." As if to confound confusion, he then proceeded to assert in his *Principles of Sociology* that the time had come when no further progress could be expected to ensue from conflicts between peoples. In the past, he declared, war had been a means whereby the earth was peopled with "the more powerful and intelligent races"; in the future, however, progress would result from "the quiet pressure of a spreading industrial civilization on a barbarism which slowly dwindles." [46] The integration of simple groups into compound and doubly compound ones by military conquest had been carried "as far as seems either practicable or desirable." But what assurance was there that it would not be carried further by natural causes? Spencer could offer none. He could only contemplate the possibility with growing alarm. [47] And if some nation, claiming to be the master race and the bearer of a higher civilization, should throw down the gauntlet to bourgeois industrial nations, would this not be perfectly natural, and would not the victory of such a nation in war validate its claim to cultural and racial superiority?

To these questions Spencer had no satisfactory answer. The truth of the matter is that his social ideal had never really been grounded in biological science, much as he liked to pretend that it was. His youthful optimism had deluded him into thinking that the historical process was moving steadily toward a free, competitive society, and his interest in the development hypothesis, combined with the omnipresent influence of the natural theology of his day, had suggested the possibility of viewing the progress of history as a simple extension of the progress of nature. But both history and biology betrayed him. The revival of militarism cast a dark shadow over the future of the free society, and Darwinian biology placed the progress of nature in an equally sombre perspective. Biological evolution no longer appeared as a steady progress of organic nature onward and upward in response to the demands of the environment but rather as a haphazard, zigzag course twisting through the whitened remains of those creatures whom the chances of heredity and environment had doomed to extinction. Social evolution took on an equally grisly and uncertain aspect. Faced with this depressing turn of events and ideas, Spencer stood his ground undaunted, somewhat disconcerted and disillusioned but little suspecting that he had helped to fashion an ideology which would be used to justify a barbarous onslaught on the free society.

The foregoing analysis of two theories of social progress does not go very far toward solving the problem of the relations between biological and social evolutionism in the nineteenth century. A few tentative conclusions would seem warranted, however, some of them drawn directly from the materials presented above, the others from more general considerations.

1. There was no necessary or inevitable connection between theories of biological evolution and theories
   of sociological evolution in the nineteenth century.
   Comte's rejection of Lamarck's development hypothesis
   should make this clear, and the same point could be
   made with respect to the social evolutionism of Marx
   and Engels.

2. Even when, as in the case of Comte, the development
   hypothesis was specifically disavowed, biological concepts and analogies often played an important role in
   social theory. Thus, Comte conceived the progress of
   the human race as a kind of temporalization of the great
   chain of being and invoked Lamarck's law of use and
   disuse to explain the evolution of human nature. Oddly
   enough, Comte, though less inclined than Spencer
   to assimilate social to biological theory, had a much
   firmer grasp of the concept of organism. Spencer never
   got beyond conceiving society as an aggregate of
   individuals.

3. The primary stimulus to speculation concerning social evolution was the growing conviction that the early condition of the human race had been a bestial one, scarcely distinguishable from that of the higher animals. This conviction sprang partly from increasing knowledge concerning the anthropoid apes but even more from growing contact with primitive cultures. It was related to biological inquiry but not specifically to evolutionary biology.

4. Given the conviction that human history was a gradual ascent from brutelike beginnings and the concomitant conviction that all natural and historical events are subject to law, it was inevitable that there should have been attempts to formulate the laws of historical development. It was inevitable, too, that these attempts should have involved heavy borrowing of concepts and principles from older fields of inquiry. In this respect Comte was much more cautious than Spencer, realizing that sociology must develop concepts appropriate to its own peculiar subject matter.

5. Finally, it was natural that the social evolutionists of the nineteenth century should have attempted to validate their programs of political and social action by claiming the sanction of science for their philosophies of history. As supernatural sanctions were discredited and the prestige of science grew, social prophets assumed the pose of the scientist. But the imposture could not long deceive. Science went on her way, a prolific but cruel mother, forever spawning scientisms and forever abandoning her illegitimate offspring.

NOTES

1. See, for example, Arthur O. Lovejoy, "Some Eighteenth Century Evolutionists," *Popular Science Monthly* 65 (1904): 238–51, 323–40; "The Supposed Primitivism of Rousseau's Discourse on Inequality," *Modern Philology* 21 (1923): 165–86; "Monboddo and

Rousseau," *Modern Philology* (1933) 30: 275–96. Also, Gladys Bryson, *Man and Society: The Scottish Inquiry of the Eighteenth Century* (Princeton, 1945); Howard Becker and Harry Elmer Barnes, *Social Thought from Lore to Science* . . ., 2nd ed. (Washington, D.C., 1952), vol. 1.

2. An exhaustive account of Comte's early years, with comprehensive bibliography, is to be found in Henri Gouhier's *La Jeunesse d'Auguste Comte et la Formation du Positivisme* 3 vols. (Paris: Bibliothèque d'Histoire de la Philosophie, 1933). See also Franck Alengry, *Essai historique et critique sur la sociologie chez Auguste Comte* (Paris, 1900).

3. Auguste Comte, *Early Essays on Social Philosophy*, trans. Henry D. Hutton (London, 1911), p. 247.

4. Ibid., p. 193, 324. See also Gouhier, *La Jeunesse d'Auguste Comte*, 1: 222.

5. Ibid., pp. 205–206.

6. Ibid., pp. 237–38.

7. Ibid., pp. 149–50. On pp. 147–48: "All men who possess a certain knowledge of the leading facts of history, be their historical views what they may, will agree in this, that the cultivated portion of the human race, considered as a whole, has made uninterrupted progress in Civilisation, from the most remote periods of history to our own day." In another passage (p. 308, n.) Comte declares that the words *improvement* and *development* are not intended to suggest "absolute excellence and indefinite amelioration" but rather "a certain succession of states which the human race reaches in accordance with fixed laws." But Comte's disclaimer of a teleological implication, like Spencer's later on, runs counter to the optimistic tenor of his writing and thinking. Neither man shared Rousseau's doubts concerning the ultimate character of human progress. Concerning human nature Comte wrote (*Early Essays*, pp. 61–62): "The majority of men desire power, when placed within their reach, not as an end but as a means. They value it, less from love of authority, than because their idleness and incapacity disposes them to employ others in procuring enjoyments instead of themselves joining in their labour. The dominant aim of almost all persons is not to act upon Man, but upon Nature."

8. *Early Essays*, 131ff., 153ff. See also Comte's *Cours de philosophie positive* (Paris, 1908) 4: 123–24, where he refers to "the evident origin of our fundamental notion of human progress, which, spontaneously issuing from the gradual development of the various positive sciences, still finds there today its most unshakable foundations."

9. Auguste Comte, *Cours* 3: 296.

10. Ibid., 3: 296—97. Although Comte rejected the development hypothesis, he had great admiration for Lamarck's other contributions, especially his classification of invertebrate animals. See also Alengry, *Essai historique*, 142ff.

11. Ibid., 3: 158. For Comte's remarks on the relation of natural history to biology, see pp. 185—86, 247—48. His conception of biology was profoundly influenced by the writings of Marie François Xavier Bichat and Henri Marie Ducrotay de Blainville. See in this connection Henri Gouhier, "La Philosophie 'Positiviste' et 'Chretienne' de D. de Blainville," *Revue philosophique* 131 (1941), pp. 38—69. See also *Cours* 3: 151ff.

12. Ibid., 3: 278—279. Comte rejected the newly proposed cell theory on the ground that it involved an attempt to reduce biology to physics and chemistry. See p. 279.

13. Ibid., 3: 301.

14. Ibid., 4: 285. See also vol. 3: 325, 403—4, 422.

15. Ibid., 4: 167. See also pp. 170, 183—85.

16. Ibid., 4: 310.

17. "It is clear, indeed, that not only political institutions properly so-called but social customs on the one hand and the *mores* and ideas on the other are reciprocally solidary and that this entire ensemble is connected constantly by its very nature to the corresponding state of integral development of humanity considered in all its various modes of activity whatever, intellectual, moral, and physical, concerning which no political system, whether temporal or spiritual, could ever have any other real aim than to regularize suitably the spontaneous activity in order to direct it better toward a more perfect accomplishment of its natural, previously determined end." *Ibid.*, 4: 176.

18. Ibid., 3: 156.

19. Ibid., 4: 201. In Comte's opinion, man was the most modifiable of all animals. One of his objections to Lamarck's development hypothesis was that it seemed to imply a higher degree of variability in the lower animals than in man. See *Cours*, 3: 297—98.

20. Ibid., 4: 329, 341, 374; 6: 506, 511—12, 515—16. On pp. 511—12: "In every degree on the sociological scale and in all its statical and dynamical relations, biology necessarily furnishes concerning human nature, insofar as it can be known by considering the individual alone, the fundamental notions which must always

control the direct findings of sociological exploration and even correct and perfect them. Moreover, in the lower part of the series, without descending to the initial state in which biological deductions alone can guide us, it is clear that biology, although always dominated . . . by the sociological spirit, must especially make known that elementary association, spontaneous intermediary between purely individual existence and a full social existence, which results from domestic existence properly so called, more or less common to all the higher animals, and which constitutes in our species the true primordial base of the larger collective organism. However, the original elaboration of this new science [sociology] must be essentially dynamical in view of the fact that the laws of harmony have there almost always been considered implicitly as laws of succession, the clear appreciation of which could alone constitute social physics today. Also, its highest scientific connection with biology consists now in the fundamental link which I have established between the sociological series and the biological series and which permits envisaging philosophically the first as a simple, gradual prolongation of the second, although the terms of the one are coexistent and those of the other successive. Except for this unique general difference, which does not prevent connecting the two series, we have, in effect, recognized that the essential character of human evolution results necessarily from the ever-increasing preponderance of the same higher attributes which place man at the head of the animal hierarchy. . . . One comes thus to conceive the immense organic system as actually linking the least vegetative existence to the noblest social existence by a long intermediate progression of higher and higher modes of existence whose succession, although necessarily discontinuous, is nevertheless essentially homogeneous."

21. Ibid., 4: 191. For Comte's views on the action of climate, race, etc. in accelerating or retarding the normal course of social evolution, see Ibid., 4: 208–10, 332ff.

22. Herbert Spencer, *Autobiography*, 1: 201. See also David Duncan, *Life and Letters of Herbert Spencer* (New York, 1906) 2: 156ff.

23. Herbert Spencer, *Social Statics: Or, the Conditions Essential to Human Happiness Specified, and the First of Them Developed* (New York, 1882), p. 447. This edition is a reprint of the original edition of 1850. The views set forth in *Social Statics* were adumbrated in Spencer's first extensive political essay, "On the Proper Sphere of Government," published as a series of letters in *The Nonconformist* in 1842. During the rest of the decade of the forties Spencer broadened the

range of his inquiries, making excursions into biology and psychology. He was much interested in Robert Chambers's *Vestiges of the Natural History of Creation* (1844) and in the phrenological doctrines of Gall and Spurzheim. In an article in the *Philosophical Magazine* in 1844, "On the Theory of Reciprocal Dependence in the Animal and Vegetable Creations as Regards Its Bearing upon Palaeontology," he propounded the theory that the amount of oxygen in the earth's atmosphere had been steadily increasing and that there must consequently have been "a gradual change in the character of the animate creation" involving "a continual increase of the hot-blooded tribes and an apparent diminution of the cold-blooded ones."

24. Ibid., p. 79.

25. Ibid., pp. 448–49.

26. Ibid., pp. 80, 447–48, 467. Like Comte, Spencer regarded the progressive complication of social institutions as analogous to the progressive gradation of living forms in nature. Unlike Comte, however, he viewed both types of complication as products of temporal evolution. See *Social Statics*, pp. 480–81, 493.

27. Ibid., p. 384.

28. Ibid., pp. 413, 426–27.

29. Ibid., p. 119.

30. Ibid., p. 29.

31. Letter from Herbert Spencer to Edward Lott, dated April 23, 1852, as quoted in Duncan, *Life and Letters*, 1: 80–81.

32. Herbert Spencer, "A Theory of Population, Deduced from the General Law of Animal Fertility," *The Westminster Review* 57 (1852): 498–99.

33. Ibid., pp. 499–500.

34. Ibid., p. 501.

35. Herbert Spencer, *The Principles of Psychology* (London, 1855), p. 529. Spencer first openly espoused the development hypothesis in a brief article in *The Leader* in March, 1852. Shortly thereafter he came across Von Baer's description of embryological development as a passage from homogeneity to heterogeneity and seized upon it as a clue to the character of organic development generally. In 1858 he attacked Richard Owen's theory of ideal types and defended the nebular hypothesis. In the following year he launched into the field of botany with an essay on the modification of leaf forms by the action of environmental forces, adducing evidence suggesting "that

the forms of all organisms are dependent on their relations to incident forces," the hereditary type changing slowly in response to the continued action of these forces. A few months later appeared his review of Hugh Miller's geological works, devoted to proving that the discontinuities in the paleontological record were not conclusive against the development hypothesis. In private conversations with Huxley, too, he pressed his favorite conception, but without success. See the *Autobiography*, 1: 445ff.; 2: 321–22. Also, Herbert Spencer, *Illustrations of Universal Progress; A Series of Discussions* (New York, 1878), in which many of the articles referred to above are reprinted.

36. Ibid., pp. 526–27. Again, page 581: "Every one of the countless connections among the fibres of the cerebral masses answers to some permanent connection of phenomena in the experiences of the race."

37. See Spencer's *Illustrations of Universal Progress*, cited above.

38. Herbert Spencer, "Progress: Its Law and Cause," ibid., p. 58.

39. Herbert Spencer, *The Study of Sociology* (New York, 1881), pp. 52–53.

40. Herbert Spencer, *The Principles of Sociology* (New York, 1877), 1: 600.

41. "The change from the homogeneous to the heterogeneous is displayed equally in the progress of civilization as a whole, and in the progress of every tribe or nation; and is still going on with increasing rapidity." See "Progress: Its Law and Cause," *Illustrations of Universal Progress*, p. 12. In this same essay Spencer attempted to strip the idea of progress of its teleological implications, but his description of progress as a "beneficent necessity" indicated that he still thought of the world process as fraught with good for mankind. See p. 58.

42. Herbert Spencer, *Principles of Sociology*, 1: 106–8.

43. Ibid., 1: 43.

44. "Doubtless, from all that has been said it follows that, if surrounding conditions remain the same, the evolution of a society cannot be in any essential way diverted from its course; though it also follows . . . that the beliefs and actions of individuals, being natural factors that arise in the course of the evolution itself, and aid in further advancing it, must be severally valued as increments of the aggregate force producing change. . . . For though the process of social evolution is so far pre-determined that no teaching or

discipline can advance it beyond a certain normal rate, which is limited by the rate of organic modification in human beings; yet it is quite possible to perturb, to retard, or to disorder the process. The analogy of individual development again serves us. . . . Growth and development may be, and often are, hindered or deranged, though they cannot be artificially bettered. Similarly with the social organism. Though, by maintaining the required conditions, there cannot be more good done than that of letting social progress go on unhindered; yet immense mischief may be done in the way of disturbing and distorting and repressing, by policies carried out in pursuance of erroneous conceptions." *Study of Sociology*, p. 396.

45. Herbert Spencer, "Mr. Martineau on Evolution," *Various Fragments* (New York, 1908), p. 379.

46. Herbert Spencer, *Principles of Sociology*, 2: 663–64.

47. Ibid., 2: 590ff.

SUGGESTED FURTHER READING

There is an abundant literature concerning Auguste Comte, but it contains very little discussion of the relations between nineteenth-century biology and Comte's social theory. One essay bearing directly on this relationship is Barbara Haines's "The Inter-relations Between Social, Biological, and Medical Thought, 1740–1850: Saint-Simon and Comte," *British Journal of the History of Science* II (1978): 19–35. There is a good selection of Comte's writings in translation, with an "Introduction" and an extensive bibliography of relevant publications, in Gertrud Lenzer, ed., *Auguste Comte and Positivism: The Essential Writings* (New York: Harper Torchbooks, Harper & Row, 1975). See also Ronald Fletcher, *The Making of Sociology. A Study of Sociological Theory* (London: Michael Joseph, 1971), vol. 1, chap. 2: "Auguste Comte: Positive Science and Sociology: A First Synthesis," pp. 165–196.

For a general view of Spencer, especially with regard to his social theory, see J. D. Y. Peel, *Herbert Spencer: The Evolution of a Sociologist* (London: Heinemann, 1971); S. Andreski, ed., *Herbert Spencer: Structure, Function and Evolution* (London: Michael Joseph, 1971); R. L. Carneiro, ed., *The Evolution of Society: Selections from Herbert Spencer's Principles of Sociology* (Chicago: University of Chicago Press, 1967); R. L. Carneiro, "Structure, Function, and Equilibrium in the Evolutionism of Herbert Spencer," *Journal of Anthropological Research* 29 (1973): 77–95. See also Robert M. Young, "The Development of

Herbert Spencer's Concept of Evolution," *Actes du XIᵉ Congrès International d'Histoire des Sciences* (Warsaw: Nadbitka, 1967) 2: 273–278; Peter B. Medawar, "Herbert Spencer and the Law of General Evolution," in *The Art of the Soluble* (Harmondsworth: Penguin Books, 1969), pp. 45–67; Derek Freeman, "The Evolutionary Theories of Charles Darwin and Herbert Spencer," *Current Anthropology* 15 (1974): 211–238.

5

DARWIN AS A SOCIAL EVOLUTIONIST

The question of Darwin's views on social evolution has long been a controversial one. At one extreme, writers like the anthropologist Marvin Harris have represented Darwin as a Spencerian in his general outlook, accusing him of "biological Spencerism," or racial determinism. To these writers Darwin was a powerful exponent, though not the originator, of "social Darwinism"—the belief that competitive struggle between individuals, tribes, nations, and races has been the chief engine of progress in social evolution. Authors of this persuasion have not hesitated to call Darwin a "racist."[1]

At the other end of the spectrum, writers like the Australian anthropologist Derek Freeman have insisted that Darwin had nothing to do with "social Darwinism" and that his views on biological and social evolution were entirely different from those of Herbert Spencer, whose speculative methods he distrusted. Darwin, Freeman would have us believe, was an "interactionist" who "recognized that human history had long since reached a phase in which learned behavioural adaptations had become 'much more' important than genetic variables in determining social change, while still attaching importance to the nature of the brain and body of man as these evolved, in earlier times, predominantly by means of natural selection."[2]

The fifteen commentaries on Freeman's essay published in the September 1974 issue of *Current Anthropology* illustrate the wide disparity of opinions prevailing on the subject of Darwin's concept of social evolution. Ernst Mayr, George Gaylord Simpson, Carl Bajema, John Blacking, U. M. Cowgill, Santiago Genovès, Michael Ghiselin, Neven P. Lamb, and Johannes Raum support Freeman's position with few qualifications. Marvin Harris defends his own position against Freeman's attack. Charles Gillispie, John Greene, Robert Carneiro, Daniel Heyduk, and Kinji Imanishi take issue with Freeman on one or more matters of substantive importance. In the intellectual community at large the diversity of opinions concerning Darwin as a social evolutionist is no less striking.[3]

How is it possible that Darwin scholars can disagree so violently about a historical question that is presumably subject to historical inquiry and verification? Preconceived ideas and prejudices—modern antipathy to biological interpretations of human behavior, Marxist prejudice against Malthus and Spencer, the tendency of biologists to make Darwin into a patron saint unblemished by any fault of mind or character—may provide a partial explanation, but something more is involved. The main difficulty is that *The Descent of Man*, the chief source of information about Darwin's views on social evolution, is ambiguous on the point at issue. Those who view Darwin as a "social Darwinist" have no difficulty in finding passages that seem to out-Spencer Spencer in proclaiming the necessity of competitive struggle between individuals, tribes, nations, and races as a prerequisite for social progress. Perhaps the best example of such a passage is the paragraph in the "General Summary" in which Darwin asserts that man, having "advanced to his present high condition through a struggle for existence consequent on his rapid multiplication," must remain subject to a severe struggle if he is to advance still further.

> Hence our natural rate of increase, though leading to many and obvious evils, must not be greatly diminished by any means. There should be open competition for all men; and the most able should not be prevented by laws or customs from succeeding best and rearing the largest number of offspring.

On the other side of the argument, there are equally striking passages in which Darwin seems to recognize the role of education, public opinion, religion, humanitarian sentiments, and social institutions generally in social evolution, especially in civilized societies. Even in precivilized societies he attributes some influence to what he calls "the standard of excellence" prevailing in each society. It is not surprising, then, that readers of *The Descent of Man* have drawn different conclusions about Darwin's views on social evolution. Darwin seems to contradict himself, leaving scholars free to draw whatever conclusions fit best with their preconceived ideas about Darwin and his role in Western thought.

It was this situation with respect to the interpretation of *The Descent of Man* that led me to search the Darwin Papers at the Cambridge University Library for evidence that might resolve the long-standing controversy. Perhaps there were early drafts of *The Descent of Man* or collections of notes gathered by Darwin for use in writing the sections on progress and retrogression in human history. But I found no such materials. It then occurred to me to examine Darwin's annotations of books and reprints in his personal library dealing with human evolution. Peter Vorzimmer's manuscript catalogues of Darwin's books and reprints lay at hand. The search for annotations began. The results proved interesting and enlightening.

The purpose of this essay is to present evidence gleaned from Darwin's annotations of books and articles concerned with human evolution and related topics and then to review his discussion of social evolution in *The Descent of Man* in the light of this new evidence. In keeping with this purpose, attention will be focused on Darwin's own statements and those of his contemporaries. A brief discussion of the implications of the new findings for the future course of Darwin studies concludes the paper. Readers interested in the extensive secondary literature on social Darwinism are referred to the bibliographies in the works by Derek Freeman and Marvin Harris cited above and to the essays by various authors in Thomas F. Glick's *The Comparative Reception of Darwinism*.[5]

For the period before 1859, Darwin's book annotations provide the main source of new information. Besides annotating the margins of pages, Darwin usually jotted comments and page references on the back flyleaf or on one or more sheets pinned to the flyleaf. Among the pre-1859 books with annotations of this kind were William Lawrence's *Lectures on*

Physiology, Zoology, and the Natural History of Man (1822); Robert Chambers's *Vestiges of the Natural History of Creation* (6th ed., 1847); Robert G. Latham's *Man and His Migrations* (1851); James Cowles Prichard's *Researches on the Physical History of Mankind* (3rd ed., 1844, and 4th ed., 1851); Lt. Col. Charles Hamilton Smith's *The Natural History of the Human Species, Its Typical Forms, Primaeval Distribution, Filiations, and Migrations* (1848); Josiah Nott and George Gliddon, *Types of Mankind* (1854); and Herbert Spencer's *Principles of Psychology* (1855). In some cases it was possible to determine exactly when Darwin read a given book from his entries in a notebook of books read.

Darwin's annotations of these books show that he was looking for evidence that the same natural agencies that disseminate, modify, improve, or bring about the decline and extinction of varieties of plants and animals had also acted on the various tribes and races of man in early human history. Thus Darwin noted on a sheet pinned to the flyleaf of Prichard's *Researches on the Physical History of Mankind*: "How like my book all this will be." For Prichard, like Darwin, attempted to throw light on the origin and development of human races by gathering information on processes of variation in plants and animals generally, arguing by analogy to the case of man. In his annotations Darwin showed particular interest in passages concerning the distribution and migrations of plants and animals, sexual selection, Buffon's ideas on the aversion of species to crossing with each other, diseases like plica polonica peculiar to particular races or nations, the effects of racial intermixture, and geographic barriers opposing the extension of Mediterranean influences into central Africa. "If I ever consider Man," Darwin reminded himself, "look over other and earlier edition."

Latham's *Man and His Migrations* was of interest to Darwin for its speculations on the processes by which the human race, presumably originating in a single locality, slowly became diffused over the earth. Two ideas in particular caught Darwin's attention. The first was Latham's distinction between the "primary diffusion," when man's dissemination was opposed only by natural obstacles, and the "secondary diffusion," when tribes encountered other tribes in their migrations. Of the primary diffusion, Darwin wrote: "N. B. the wide and rapid spreading of introduced plant is something like this—its preyers [?] are not yet developed." With respect to the secondary diffusion, Darwin took special note of Latham's description of encroachment, displacement, and obliteration of intermediate forms in the conflict of tribes and races, resulting in the geographical proximity of strikingly different types, such as the Hottentots and the Caffres in southern Africa. "Excellent remarks (quote in Ch 6?)," Darwin noted, "on how during encroachment, one race will obliterate intermediate forms: I do not see force of Displacement—If one form gains an advantage over other independent of *climate*, it will overwhelm the graduated intermediate forms."

Darwin's query—"quote in Ch 6?"—shows that he was contemplating discussing human evolution in the treatise on the origin of species on which he was working at the time he read these books. That he was seriously considering this is confirmed by a penciled notation in the table of contents of the "long version" of the *Origin of Species* recently published by Robert Stauffer under the title *Charles Darwin's Natural Selection*. This notation, which reads "Theory Applied to the Races of Man," shows that Darwin contemplated including a section in chapter 6 designed to show that his theory of natural selection was applicable to human evolution and, in particular, to the evolution of human races. The proposed section seems never to have been written, but the general nature of the argument Darwin had in mind seems clear enough from his annotations of the books in his library, several of them bearing annotations specifically labeled for use in chapter 6. These annotations show beyond question that he intended to prove that the same agencies of population pressure, struggle for existence, migration, encroachment and extinction of races and tribes, differential susceptibility to disease, and so forth, that played a central role in his theory of evolution by natural selection had shaped the early development of mankind. They also show his tendency to focus on human races as the biological equivalent in the human sphere of the varieties of plants and animals that formed the materials of evolution in the organic world generally.

The centrality of race formation in Darwin's concept of human evolution comes out in the title—"Theory Applied to the Races of Man"—of the projected section of chapter 6. It is also apparent in his letter to Charles Lyell dated October 11, 1859, in which Darwin wrote:

> I suppose that you do not doubt that the intellectual powers are as important for the welfare of each being as corporeal structure; if so, I can see no difficulty in the most intellectual individuals of a species being continually selected and the intellect of the new species thus improved, aided probably by effects of inherited mental exercise. I look at this process as now going on with the races of man; the less intellectual races being exterminated.[6]

He had expressed the same idea twenty years earlier in Notebook E of the transmutation notebooks he kept after his return from the voyage of the *Beagle*: "When two races of men meet, they act precisely like two species of animals—they fight, eat each other, bring diseases to each other, etc. but then comes the more deadly struggle, namely which have the best fitted organisation, or instinct (i.e. intellect in man) to gain the day."[7]

Darwin's reference to the probable effects of "inherited mental exercise" in his letter to Lyell is interesting in the light of his annotations of Herbert Spencer's *Principles of Psychology* (1855), sent to Darwin "With the Author's Compliments." On pages 547–548 of this work Spencer argued:

> Let it be granted that in all creatures, as in ourselves, the law is and ever has been, that the more frequently psychical states occur in a certain order, the stronger becomes their tendency to cohere in that order, until they at last become inseparable; let it be granted that this tendency is, in however slight a degree, inherited, so that if the experiences remain the same, each successive generation bequeathes a somewhat increased tendency; and it follows, that . . . there must inevitably be established an automatic connection of nervous actions, corresponding to the external relations perpetually experienced.

Beside Spencer's statement of the law of psychical states, Darwin wrote: ". . . is this not true for what he calls physical"? On the flyleaf Darwin commented on Spencer's derivation of the Kantian categories of pure reason from the inherited effects of the daily experience of the human race as follows: "577—583 good discussion on necessity of evolution Hypothesis to unite experience & transcendental hypothesis." Darwin was to return to the idea of the "effects of inherited mental exercise" in *The Descent of Man*.

Before leaving Darwin's pre-1859 annotations, we should note the absence in them of an idea that was to become prominent in his later writings, namely, the importance of genetically based psychological and moral differences between individuals, tribes, nations, and races in the struggle for existence. Although the books he read before 1859, especially those of William Lawrence, Spencer, and the American polygenists Nott and Gliddon, were full of passages expatiating on the supposed psychological and moral differences between tribes, nations, and races, Darwin left these passages unmarked. If he believed in the reality of genetic differences of this kind (the evidence is not clear on this point), he did not then conceive that these differences were an important factor in human evolution. In any case, he had decided not to discuss man in his *Origin of Species*. Concerning the bearing of his theory of evolution by natural selection on human evolution, he ventured only to predict that "light will be thrown on the origin of man and his history."

But if Darwin was not yet ready to expound the implications of his theory of natural selection for social evolution, the same cannot be said of his fellow countrymen. Although Darwin wrote little or nothing about man in the 1860s, his *Origin of Species* inspired innumerable books and articles in which his theory was applied to the past, present, and future development of the human race. Darwin read and annotated many of these, receiving some of them as complimentary copies and purchasing others for his own use. Among the

British writers on social evolution whose works he read and annotated were Alfred Russel Wallace, Francis Galton, Walter Bagehot, John Lubbock, Herbert Spencer, William Lecky, Edward Tylor, J. F. McLennan, W. R. Greg, and David Page. Their writings stimulated Darwin enormously, introducing new perspectives and challenging him to formulate his own views on human evolution more clearly.

In Darwin's annotations of these books and articles we see a continuation of his interest in applying the theory of natural selection to human history, but with some new emphases and problems. The first new theme occurred in his annotations of Alfred Russel Wallace's article in the *Anthropological Review* for May 1864, entitled "The Origin of Human Races and the Antiquity of Man Deduced from the Theory of 'Natural Selection'," which seems to have impressed Darwin greatly and to have led him to consider seriously the idea that natural selection acts on man's "moral faculties" as well as on his physical and intellectual capacities. Darwin marked heavily a passage in which Wallace argued that such mental and moral qualities as sympathy, capacity for acting in concert, intelligent foresight, and the like would be acted on by natural selection. "Tribes in which such mental and moral qualities were predominant," Wallace wrote, "would therefore have an advantage in the struggle for existence over other tribes in which they were less developed, would live and maintain their numbers, while the others would decrease and finally succumb." Darwin drew a double line alongside this passage and wrote in the margin: "Use of moral qualities."

More generally, Darwin appears to have resonated sympathetically to Wallace's conception of intellectual and moral progress resulting from the action of natural selection on the physical, mental, and moral capacity of individuals, tribes, nations, and races. He marked heavily Wallace's speculation that races subject to "the harsh discipline of a sterile soil and inclement seasons" would develop greater hardihood, foresight, and ingenuity than those in tropical regions and his declaration that the great law of the preservation of favored races in the struggle for life "leads to the inevitable extinction of all those low and mentally undeveloped populations with which Europeans come in contact." "The red Indian in North America, and in Brasil; the Tasmanian, Australian and New Zealander in the southern hemisphere, die out, not from any one special cause, but from the inevitable effects of an unequal mental and physical struggle." Darwin drew a double line beside this passage and wrote at the top of the page: "natural selection is now acting on the inferior races when put into competition with the New Zealanders—high [?] New Zelander [sic] say the race dying out like their own native rat."[8]

Darwin also underlined Wallace's statement that, owing to natural selection of even the slightest variations in man's mental and moral nature, "the better and higher specimens of our race would therefore increase and spread, the lower and more brutal would give way and successively die out, and that rapid advancement of mental organisation would occur, which has raised the very lowest races of man so far above the brutes, (although differing so little from some of them in physical structure), and, in conjunction with scarcely perceptible modifications of form, has developed the wonderful intellect of the Germanic races." Darwin seems to have intended quoting this passage in a work of his own, but he crossed out the final reference to the development of the "wonderful intellect of the Germanic races." Wallace, when he reprinted this essay in 1870, changed the word "Germanic" to "European," presumably because Bismarck's unification of Germany by blood and iron had made the Germanic intellect seem less wonderful than it had in 1864.

From Darwin's correspondence with Wallace we know that Darwin had a very high opinion of his friend's essay of 1864. "The great leading idea is quite new to me, viz. that during late ages the mind will have been modified more than the body," Darwin wrote to Wallace on May 28, 1864; "yet I had got as far as to see with you that the struggle between the races of man depended entirely on intellectual and moral qualities. The latter part of the paper I can designate only as grand and most eloquently done. I have shown your paper to two or three persons who have been here, and they have been equally struck with it."[9] In another letter to Wallace on

January 26, 1870, Darwin called the essay of 1864 "the best paper that ever appeared in the Anthropological Review!" As for the latter part of the paper, in which Wallace predicted the triumph of "the more intellectual and moral" races over the "lower and more degraded" ones and which seemed to Darwin "grand and most eloquently done," it is worth noting that Wallace's footnote gave credit for the ideas expounded there to his reading of Herbert Spencer's *Social Statics*.

If Darwin had any doubt about the heritability of mental and moral capacities and dispositions, it was effectively removed when he read Francis Galton's articles on "Hereditary Talent and Character" in *Macmillan's Magazine* in June and August 1865. As examples of hereditary moral dispositions Galton listed "craving for drink, or for gambling, strong sexual passion, a proclivity to pauperism, to crimes of violence, and to crimes of fraud." But Darwin seems to have been especially impressed by Galton's comparison of the psychological and moral characteristics of various races. According to Galton, the American Indian is cold, melancholic, patient, and taciturn, with a strong sense of personal dignity. Negroes, on the contrary, are warm-hearted, gregarious, domestic, prolific, impulsive, and vociferous, but lacking in patience, reticence, and dignity. Darwin marked this comparison and wrote in the margin of the page: "This is strong [?] evidence of inheritance of all sorts of mental dispositions." Later on, in his *Variation of Animals and Plants under Domestication*, Darwin wrote: "Some writers have doubted whether those complex mental attributes, on which genius and talent depend, are inherited. . . . But he who will read Mr. Galton's able paper on hereditary talent will have his doubts allayed."[10]

Galton also reinforced Wallace's idea that natural selection favors tribes in which the affections (sexual, parental, filial, and social) are strongest. "Those who possessed all of them, in the strongest measure, would, speaking generally, have an advantage in the struggle for existence," Galton wrote. In particular, Darwin marked for quotation in chapters 3 and 4 of *The Descent of Man* Galton's observation that disinterested feelings were more necessary to man than to any other animal because of the length of his dependency in childhood, his great social needs, and his physical helplessness. "Darwin's law of natural selection would therefore be expected to develop these sentiments among men, even among the lowest barbarians, to a greater degree than among animals," Galton concluded.

Darwin also drew from Galton a historical example of natural selection of psychological and moral traits: the case of English emigrants to America. These emigrants, said Galton, were "bred from the most restless and combative class of Europe." "Every head of an emigrant family brought with him a restless character, and a spirit apt to rebel. . . . They [the Americans] are enterprising, defiant, touchy, impatient of authority; furious politicians; very tolerant of fraud and violence; possessing much high and general spirit, and some true religious feeling, but strongly addicted to cant." Darwin was to express related views in *The Descent of Man* (see below).

A second theme that caught Darwin's attention in these articles was Galton's concern with negative selection—the survival of the "unfit"—in civilized societies. Darwin had certainly been aware of this aspect of social evolution before he read Galton—he had marked a passage dealing with this problem in William Lawrence's *Lectures on Physiology, Zoology, and the Natural History of Man* many years earlier—but he seems not to have felt the full force of the problem until it was given a central place by Galton, W. R. Greg, and others in the 1860s. An early eugenicist, Galton was convinced that only some kind of eugenic control could counteract the tendency of civilization to weaken society by preventing natural selection from eliminating its weak and intellectually inferior members.

> If a twentieth part of the cost and pains were spent in measures for the improvement of the human race that is spent on the improvement of the breed of horses and cattle [Galton wrote], what a galaxy of genius might we not create! . . .
> The feeble nations of the world are necessarily giving way before the nobler varieties of mankind; and even the best of these, so far as we know them, seem unequal to their work. The

average culture of mankind is become so much higher than it was, and the branches of knowledge and history so various and extended, that few are capable even of comprehending the exigencies of our modern civilization; much less fulfilling them. We are living in a sort of intellectual anarchy, for the want of master minds. The general intellectual capacity of our leaders requires to be raised, and also to be differentiated.[11]

Darwin seems to have been impressed by Galton's discussion of the deleterious effects of negative selection in civilized nations, for he marked a passage of this kind in Galton's second article and made a note to himself to refer to it in chapter 4 of *The Descent of Man*, where, in fact, he cites Galton and echoes some of his views:

the weak members of civilised societies propagate their kind. No one who has attended to the breeding of domestic animals will doubt that this must be highly injurious to the race of man. It is surprising how soon a want of care, or care wrongly directed, leads to the degeneration of a domestic race; but excepting in the case of man himself, hardly any one is so ignorant as to allow his worst animals to breed.[12]

Thus Galton's essay, coming hard on the heels of Wallace's article of 1864, seems to have strengthened Darwin's belief that mental and moral capacities and dispositions were heritable and that natural selection had acted on them throughout history in the competition of individuals, tribes, nations, and races. On the one hand, natural selection had operated to strengthen the social and sympathetic feelings among men. On the other, these feelings had acted to inhibit the operation of natural selection in civilized societies, thereby posing a threat to the continued progress of mankind. Here was a dilemma Darwin was to wrestle with in *The Descent of Man* without achieving a resolution.

In September 1868 the problem of the survival of the "unfit" in civilized societies was posed again for Darwin by an anonymous article in *Fraser's Magazine* entitled "On the Failure of 'Natural Selection' in the Case of Man." The author, as Darwin later discovered, was a Scotsman named William R. Greg, an essayist and frequent contributor to the

British quarterlies. Like Wallace, Galton, and other British writers, Greg was concerned with the implications of Darwin's theory of natural selection for the progress of civilization. In passages heavily lined by Darwin, Greg paraphrased Wallace's description of the process by which natural selection had slowly perfected man's body, mind, and moral faculties in the course of human evolution, dilating on "the great wise, righteous, and beneficent principle which in all other animals, and in man himself, up to a certain stage of his progress, tends to the improvement and perfection of the race."

But what had happened to the operation of this principle as man became civilized? According to Greg, the "righteous and salutary law of 'natural selection' " was still operative in the competition between the races of man:

> Here the abler, the stronger, the more advanced, the finer in short, are still the favoured ones, succeed in the competition; exterminate, govern, supersede, fight, eat, or work the inferior tribes out of existence. The process is quite as certain, and nearly as rapid, whether we are just or unjust; whether we use carefulness or cruelty. Everywhere the savage tribes of mankind die out at the contact of the civilised ones.[13]

So too, in most cases, in the struggle for existence among nations. "In the dawn of history the more cultivated and energetic races conquered the weaker and less advanced, reduced them to slavery, or taught them civilisation." True, the Romans conquered the intellectually superior Greeks, but the Greeks by this time had become "enervated and corrupt to the very cores" and so fell victim to "the robuster will and unequalled political genius of their Roman conquerors," who were "morally and *volitionally* more vigorous." The Romans, in their turn, succumbed to rude Northern warriors who "brought with them a renovating irruption of that hard energy and redundant vitality which luxury and success had nearly extinguished among those they conquered."

Darwin's pencil, which had been busy underlining these passages and making brief notes in the margins, continued active as Greg explained the rise and fall of various European peoples—Italians, Spaniards, Frenchmen, Englishmen—in terms of their supposed intellectual and moral endowments. France had won her vast influence by "her wonderful military spirit and the peculiarity of her singularly clear, keen, restless, but not rich intelligence." England owed her worldwide dominion to "a *daring and persistent energy* [Darwin's underlining] with which no other variety of mankind is largely dowered." And if, in these struggles, might seemed sometimes to have triumphed over right, it was "because in the counsels of the Most High, energy is seen to be more needed than culture to carry on the advancement of humanity, and a commanding will, at least in this stage of our progress, a more essential endowment than an amiable temper or a good heart." In any case, Greg concluded, "it is those who in some sense are the strongest and fittest who most prevail, multiply, and spread, and become in the largest measure the progenitors of future nations."

Having proved to his own satisfaction the beneficent action of natural selection in the competition of nations and races, Greg turned to the main theme of his essay, namely, the failure of natural selection at the level of individuals and classes in a community. Darwin followed closely, pencil in hand. Greg's main argument in this section was that the middle classes—"those who form the energetic, reliable, improving element of the population, those who wish to rise and do not choose to sink, those in a word who are the true strength and wealth and dignity of nations"—tend to have fewer children than the rich and the poor, both of whom "marry as early as they please and have as many children as they please—the rich because it is in their power, the poor because they have no motive for abstinence." Darwin seems to have had reservations about this argument, for his annotation reads: ". . . do these extremes exceed so much in number the *marrying* middle classes [?]." But he was sufficiently impressed by Greg's comparison of "the careless, squalid, unaspiring Irishman, fed on potatoes, living in a pig-stye, doting on a superstition, [who] multiplies like rabbits or ephemera" with "the frugal, foreseeing, self-respecting, ambitious Scot, stern in his morality, spiritual in his faith, sagacious and disciplined in his intelligence, [who] passes his best years in struggle and celibacy, marries late, and leaves few behind him" to clip out this passage and quote it verbatim in *The Descent of Man* as an example of negative selection in civilized societies.

Clearly, Darwin was stimulated by Greg's article. He marked it "Keep" and followed the controversy that it evoked in the British press, annotating some of the replies. He appears to have written Galton about it, for on January 28, 1870, Galton wrote him: "Greg did write the article in Fraser, and has no objection at all—but the contrary—in being publickly spoken of as the author. He is highly gratified at your appreciation of the article."[14] Yet Darwin was not entirely convinced by Greg's arguments. Beside the statement of the main thesis—"that the indisputable effect of the state of social progress and culture we have reached . . . is to counteract and suspend the operation of that righteous and salutary law of 'natural selection' in virtue of which the best specimens of the race   succeed . . . and propagate an ever improving and perfecting type of humanity"—Darwin wrote: "We only *counteract* it. But is there any compensation[?]". At the end of the essay, where Greg concludes that "a race is being run between moral and mental enlightenment and the deterioration of the physical constitution through the defeasance of the law of natural selection," Darwin gave no clear indication of his own position. "Humanity and good feeling encouraged," he wrote at the bottom of the page, but the reference of this cryptic remark is not clear.

Shortly before he read Greg's article, Darwin read and annotated two essays by Walter Bagehot on "Physics and Politics," published in *The Fortnightly Review* for November 1, 1867, and April 1, 1868. In these essays Bagehot combined Spencer's concept of the inherited effects of daily activities on the nervous system, Darwin's theory of natural selection, and some theories of his own to explain social evolution. Progress, he insisted in a passage marked by Darwin, was neither necessary or normal in human history. Among primitive men the "cake of custom," subjecting individuals to group norms and instilling the habit of implicit obedience, had to be formed before political organization was possible:

> what makes one tribe—one incipient tribe, one bit of a tribe—to differ from another is *their relative faculty* [Darwin's italics] of coherence. The slightest symptom of legal development, the least indication of a military bond, is then enough to turn the scale. The compact tribes win, and the compact tribes are the tamest. Civilisation begins, because the beginning of civilisation is a military advantage. [15]

Darwin seems to have liked this argument, for he made a note—"457 coherence"—on the last page of the article. Perhaps he was reminded of Galton's emphasis on the selective importance of affections making for social solidarity. He also underlined Bagehot's quotation from "Captain Galton" to the effect that the wild members of every flock tend to be lost or slaughtered, leaving the tame animals to "bequeath their domestic aptitudes to the future herd."

But if rigid conformity and adherence to tradition were prerequisite for the achievement of a civilized state, how was social progress possible? It came about primarily, said Bagehot, through conflict between tribes, nations, and races, resulting in racial mixtures some of which produced "beneficial variability."

> In the early world many mixtures must have wrought many ruins; they must have destroyed what they could not replace—an inbred principle of discipline and order. But if these unions of races did not work thus, if, for example, the two races were so near akin that their morals united as well as their breeds, if one race by its great numbers and prepotent organisation so presided over the other as to take it up and assimilate it, and leave no separate remains of it, *then* [Darwin's italics] the admixture was invaluable. It added to the probability of variability, and therefore of improvement; and if that improvement even in part took the military line, it might give the mixed and ameliorated state a steady advantage in the battle of nations, and a greater chance of lasting in the world. [16]

Darwin was interested in this argument, as his underlining of the words "beneficial variability" in a similar passage shows. The subject of racial mixtures was very much on his mind at this time in connection with his work on *The Variation of Animals and Plants under Domestication*. In that work he speculated on the possible deleterious effects of racial mixtures as follows:

> When two races, both low in the scale, are crossed, the progeny seems to be eminently bad. Thus the noble-hearted Humboldt, who felt none of that prejudice against the inferior races now so current in England, speaks in strong terms of the bad and savage disposition of Zambos, or half-castes between Indians and Negroes; and this conclusion has been arrived at by various observers. From these facts we may perhaps infer that the degraded state of so many half-castes is in part due to reversion to a primitive and savage condition, induced by the act of crossing, as well as to the unfavorable moral conditions under which they generally exist.[17]

What Darwin thought of Bagehot's notion that racial mixtures might occasionally produce beneficial variations capable of counteracting the inertial tendency of stable societies is not clear, but he underscored Bagehot's exposition of the "terrible sanctions" which, in arrested civilizations like those of the Orient, "killed out of the whole society the propensities to variation which were the principle of progress," and wrote in the margin: "nations which *wander* & cross would be most likely to vary."

Darwin also showed great interest in Bagehot's discussion of the positive and negative effects of selection by war and military conquest. On the whole, Bagehot was inclined to stress the positive effects. Conceding that war did not nourish humanitarian sentiments and respect for human rights, he nevertheless concluded that the "preliminary virtues"—valor, veracity, the spirit of obedience, the habit of discipline—had been essential to the progress of the human race, especially in the early stages of civilization. "Any of these, and of others like them, when possessed by a nation, and no matter how generated, will give them a military advantage, and make them more likely to *stay* in the race of nations." Darwin was to return to this question in *The Descent of Man*.

All in all, Darwin seems to have found much food for

thought in Bagehot's essays. "If you had time," he wrote to Joseph Dalton Hooker, "you ought to read an article by W. Bagehot in the April number of the *Fortnightly*, applying Natural Selection to early or prehistoric politics, and, indeed, to late politics—this you know is your view."[18] Though he attributed the idea to Hooker, Darwin himself was interested in applying the theory of natural selection to history. He underlined, no doubt with some satisfaction, Bagehot's observation that "as every great scientific conception tends to advance its boundaries and to be of use in solving problems not thought of when it was started, so here, what was put forward for mere animal history may, with a change of form, but an identical essence, be applied to human history." In *The Descent of Man* Darwin would echo several of Bagehot's assertions: that progress is not inevitable or even usual in human societies, that any form of polity is better than none, that military conflict has negative as well as positive effects on human progress. He may also have drawn unconsciously on Bagehot's theory of social imitation in developing his own concept of the role of "standards of excellence" in the progress of civilization. Bagehot applied this theory primarily in explaining the origins of national character: "At first a sort of 'chance predominance' made a model, and then invincible attraction, the necessity which rules all but the strongest men to imitate what is before their eyes, and to be what they are expected to be, moulded men to that model." Finally, Bagehot echoed Galton in speculating that the "eager restlessness" and "highly-strung nervous organizations" of the Anglo-Americans were "useful in continual struggle, and also . . . promoted by it." Here again Darwin concurred.

　　Still further light is thrown on the development of Darwin's views on social evolution by his annotations of a little-known work entitled *Man: Where, Whence, and Whither. Being a Glance at Man in His Natural-History Relations*, published in Edinburgh in 1867. The author, David Page, was a Fellow of the Royal Society of Edinburgh and of the Geological Society and author of several books on geology and paleontology. Apparently, Darwin once planned to quote various parts of this book, for several page references are listed on the inside of the back cover with a large *Q* beside them, but he subsequently changed his mind and drew a large X through the whole.

Page's main thesis was that the progress of civilization had been brought about by the successive emergence of new and higher races in the struggle for existence, "the later from the earlier, the higher from the lower, and the lower from those next beneath them." First came the Negro, then the Malay, the American Indian, and the Mongol, and finally the Caucasian. "The higher and advancing has ever passed over the inferior and stationary; the older and effete must ever make way for the recent and vigorous. The whole history of mankind is but a record of aggression and subjugation, of progress and extinction."[19] The progressive improvement of the human race through the competition of nations and races would continue into the future, Page predicted. "In virtue of the great law of cosmical progression, the white will be superseded by higher varieties, and the man of the future will excel the man of the present, even more than the most exalted European philosopher excels the wretched Bushman or Andamaner."

One suspects that Darwin responded sympathetically to passages like these. Had he not written Lyell several years earlier that "the white man is 'improving off the face of the earth' even races nearly his equal" and confessed that it would give him "infinite satisfaction" to believe that his generation would be regarded as "mere Barbarians" in a remotely distant future?[20] Whatever the case, Darwin marked the passage in which Page recited the catalogue of peoples— Chaldeans, Phoenicians, Hebrews, Pelasgians, Greeks, Romans, Moors, Celts, Franks, and Anglo-Saxons—who had successively made their mark upon history, jotting a reminder to himself—"171 Extinction of old civilizations"—in the back of the book. He also drew a line and wrote "refer to" in the margin beside the following passage, which concluded Page's account of the successive triumphs of ever nobler races in the march of human progress:

> Bound by the obligations of enlightened humanity, the white man may and must endeavour to civilise and ameliorate the condition of his less enlightened and coloured brethren; but no humanising scheme, however anxious or earnest, can ever arrest

that law which has destined the progression of the human race—
the extinction of the inferior, and the rise and spread of the
higher varieties. Humanly speaking, it is only in this way that
the progressive advancement of mankind can ever be attained;
rationally, it is the only method the human mind can comprehend and appreciate.[21]

So far as I know, Darwin never referred to this passage in
his writings, but it may well have been in the back of his mind
when, in writing *The Descent of Man*, he struggled to reconcile
his conviction that competition between individuals, tribes,
nations, and races was essential to the progress of mankind
with his equally strong sense of "the obligations of enlightened humanity" toward peoples "lower in the scale" of
human existence.

In chapters 4 and 5 of *The Descent of Man* the results of
Darwin's reflection on these and other books and articles he
had read and annotated were set forth at considerable length.
Ever since the publication of the *Origin of Species*, speculation
had been rife concerning the bearing of Darwin's theory of
natural selection on the evolution of man and society. "Light
will be thrown on the origin of man and his history," Darwin
had predicted. Now it was time for Darwin himself to shed
light on this all-absorbing question.

In general, Darwin recognized three kinds of influences in
human evolution: (1) the action of natural selection on man's
physical, intellectual, and moral faculties; (2) the inherited
effects of mental and moral exercise; and (3) the influence of
social institutions, public opinion, and other cultural factors.
In the case of precivilized societies, he assigned predominant
influence to natural selection, aided by the inherited effects of
mental and moral training and activity. As to the "intellectual
faculties," he wrote:

> We can see, that in the rudest state of society, the individuals
> who were the most sagacious, who invented and used the best
> weapons or traps, and who were best able to defend themselves,
> would rear the greatest number of offspring. . . . The stature and
> strength of the men of a tribe are likewise of some importance
> for its success, and these depend in part on the nature and

amount of the food which can be obtained. In Europe the men of the Bronze period were supplanted by a race more powerful, and, judging from their sword-handles, with larger hands; but their success was probably still more due to superiority in the arts. . . . At the present day civilised nations are everywhere supplanting barbarous nations, excepting where the climate opposes a deadly barrier; and they succeed mainly, though not exclusively, through their arts, which are the products of the intellect. It is, therefore, highly probable that with mankind the intellectual faculties have been mainly and gradually perfected through natural selection; and this conclusion is sufficient for our purpose.[22]

Darwin here appears to interpret superiority in "the arts" (technology) as evidence of innate intellectual superiority, which, in turn, is viewed as the product of natural selection. This is in keeping with the view expressed in his letter to Lyell in 1859: "I can see no difficulty in the most intellectual individuals of a species being continually selected and the intellect of the new species thus improved, aided probably by effects of inherited mental exercise. I look at this process as now going on with the races of man; the less intellectual races being exterminated."

Darwin noted, however, that, "as the progenitors of man became social," the intellectual powers would be increased and modified through imitation and the inherited effects of mental activity as well as by natural selection. The interplay of these various influences is described as follows:

Now, if some one man in a tribe, more sagacious than the others, invented a new snare or weapon, or other means of attack or defence, the plainest self-interest . . . would prompt the other members to imitate him; and all would thus profit. The habitual practice of each new art must likewise in some slight degree strengthen the intellect. If the new invention were an important one, the tribe would increase in number, spread, and supplant other tribes. In a tribe thus rendered more numerous there would always be a rather greater chance of the birth of other superior and inventive members. If such men left children to inherit their mental superiority, the chance of the birth of still more ingenious members would be somewhat better, and in a small tribe decidedly better. Even if they left no children, the tribe would still include their blood-relations; and it has been ascertained by agriculturists that by preserving and breeding from the family of an animal, which when slaughtered was found to be valuable, the desired character has been obtained.[23]

Here again, the emphasis is on natural selection of the most intelligent individuals, the multiplication of the tribe through its superiority in technology, and the consequent increase in the chances of producing "other superior and inventive members." The habitual practice of the newly invented arts provides an auxiliary source of intellectual improvement.

As for man's "social and moral faculties," such as sympathy, fidelity, and courage, these too, Darwin conjectured, "were no doubt acquired . . . through natural selection, aided by inherited habit."

> Obedience, as Mr. Bagehot has well shewn, is of the highest value, for any form of government is better than none. Selfish and contentious people will not cohere, and without coherence nothing can be effected. A tribe rich in the above qualities would spread and be victorious over other tribes. But in the course of time it would, judging from all past history, be in its turn overcome by some other tribe still more highly endowed. Thus the social and moral qualities would tend slowly to advance and be diffused throughout the world.[24]

Darwin even tried to envisage the steps by which the number of morally well-endowed men might increase in certain tribes. The habit of aiding one's fellow tribesmen, he reasoned, might originate from an expectation of receiving their aid in return. This habit, practiced through many generations, would tend to be inherited. More important still, public opinion within the tribe would strongly reinforce socially desirable modes of behavior and discourage nonsocial ones. In the long run, the increase in the number of well-endowed men and the steady advance in the standard of morality would give the tribes undergoing these changes victory over other tribes, "and this would be natural selection." "At all times throughout the world tribes have supplanted other tribes; and as morality is one important element in their success, the standard of morality and the number of well-endowed men will thus everywhere tend to rise and increase."[25]

That "moral faculties", like intellectual abilities, were heritable Darwin had no doubt, but whether the effects of moral training were also heritable was a question on which he was less sure. In *The Descent of Man* he quoted the dictum of "our great philosopher" Herbert Spencer that "the experiences of the human race, have been producing corresponding modifications, which, by continued transmission and accumulation, have become in us certain faculties of moral intuition," and commented as follows:

> There is not the least inherent improbability, as it seems to me, in virtuous tendencies being more or less strongly inherited; for, not to mention the various dispositions and habits transmitted by many of our domestic animals to their offspring, I have heard of authentic cases in which a desire to steal and a tendency to lie appeared to run in families of the upper ranks. . . . Except through the principle of the transmission of moral tendencies, we cannot understand the differences believed to exist in this respect between the various races of mankind.[26]

Darwin was cautious on this point. He wrote "believed to exist" rather than "existing" and noted that the strong moral aversion to "unclean" food in certain religious sects was not inherited. He concluded, however, that virtuous tendencies, at least in some cases, were probably heritable and that "they become first impressed on the mental organization through habit, instruction and example, continued during several generations in the same family, and in a quite subordinate degree, or not at all, by the individuals possessing such virtues having succeeded best in the struggle for life." This discussion, strongly reminiscent of similar passages in Galton's essays on "Hereditary Talent and Character," ends on a strongly optimistic note. The social instincts, established by natural selection and strengthened by reason, habit, instruction and example, will gradually become more tender and widely diffused, "extending to men of all races, to the imbecile, maimed, and other useless members of society, and finally to the lower animals," as the standard of morality rises higher and higher.

> Looking to future generations, there is no cause to fear that the social instincts will grow weaker, and we may expect that virtuous habits will grow stronger, becoming perhaps fixed by inheritance. In this case the struggle between our higher and lower impulses will be less severe, and virtue will be triumphant. [27]

In chapter 5 Darwin made the transition from precivilized to civilized societies and discussed the causes of progress and retrogression in recorded history. Progress, he observed on the authority of Bagehot and Sir Henry Maine, is not normal in human society. In primeval times it came about chiefly through the action of natural selection on man's intellectual and moral faculties in the struggle for existence. (Here Darwin cites Wallace's "admirable paper" of 1864.) In civilized societies, however, the action of natural selection is greatly diminished by the spread of humanitarian sentiments that tend to prevent the speedy elimination of the weak, the sick, the malformed, the incompetent, and other "useless" members of society. Here Darwin plunged into a discussion of negative selection in civilized society, explicitly acknowledging his debt to Wallace, Galton, and Greg. Declaring his own conviction that the humanitarian impulses of civilized man cannot be curbed without injuring "the noblest part of our nature," he went on to argue that natural selection was still operative to some degree in civilized societies and that progress or retrogression in a given society depended to a great extent on the balance between the "downward tendency" of negative selection and the positive factors counteracting it.

> If the various checks [on this downward tendency] . . . do not prevent the reckless, the vicious and otherwise inferior members of society from increasing at a quicker rate than the better class of men, the nation will retrograde, as has too often occurred in the history of the world. It is very difficult to say why one civilised nation rises, becomes more powerful, and spreads more widely, than another. We can only say that it depends on an increase in the actual number of the men endowed with high

intellectual and moral faculties, as well as on their standard of excellence. Corporeal structure appears to have little influence, except so far as vigour of body leads to vigour of mind.[28]

In the ensuing paragraphs Darwin applied this general thesis to the development of Western civilization, citing the arguments of Galton, Lyell, Greg, and others in his footnotes. With Galton and Lyell he maintained that the practice of celibacy in the Middle Ages had had "a deteriorating influence on each successive generation" and that the Inquisition had retarded progress by removing from the reproductive pool the freest and boldest men—"those who doubted and questioned, and without doubting there can be no progress." Like Galton, Bagehot, and Page, he attributed the "wonderful progress" of the United States and the character of its people to the operation of natural selection, endorsing the view of the Rev. Foster Zincke that: "All other series of events—as that which resulted in the culture of mind in Greece, and that which resulted in the empire of Rome—only appear to have purpose and value when viewed in connection with, or rather as subsidiary to . . . the great stream of Anglo-Saxon emigration to the west."

Darwin recognized, however, that natural selection was not the sole and sufficient explanation of progress and retrogression in civilized societies. If that were the case, the Greeks, "who stood some grades higher in intellect than any race that has ever existed," would have conquered their neighbors and spread throughout Europe. Their failure to do so Darwin interpreted as evidence that natural selection was but one of several factors at work. "The Greeks may have retrograded from a want of coherence between the many small states, from the size of their whole country, from the practice of slavery, or from extreme sensuality; for they did not succumb until 'they were enervated and corrupt to the very core.'"

Thus Darwin attempted to balance the influence of purely cultural factors in social evolution against the long-run effects of natural selection in the struggle for existence. During most of human history, he was convinced, natural selection had played the dominant role: "Had he [man] not been subjected during primeval times to natural selection, assuredly he would never have attained to his present rank." In civilized societies, however, natural selection played a smaller role, "for such nations do not supplant and exterminate one another as do savage tribes." "The more efficient causes of progress seem to consist of a good education during youth whilst the brain is impressible, and of a high standard of excellence, inculcated by the ablest and best men, embodied in the laws, customs and traditions of the nations, and enforced by public opinion."[29] But natural selection was still at work, even in civilized nations. The more intelligent members of such nations would be more successful than the inferior members and leave a more numerous progeny. In the long run, Darwin concluded, "a nation which produced during a lengthened period the greatest number of highly intellectual, energetic, brave, patriotic, and benevolent men, would generally prevail over less favored nations." And those people, like the Spaniards in South America, who had ceased to be subject to a severe struggle for existence would tend to become indolent and retrograde.

So it was in Darwin's "General Summary" at the end of *The Descent of Man.* On the one hand, he stressed the predominant influence of "habit, the reasoning powers, instruction, religion, &c.," in improving the "moral qualities," which constituted "the highest part of man's nature." On the other, he insisted on the necessity of a "severe struggle" if mankind was to advance still further instead of sinking into indolence: "our natural rate of increase, though leading to many and obvious evils, must not be greatly diminished by any means. There should be open competition for all men; and the most able should not be prevented by laws or customs from succeeding best and rearing the largest number of offspring."[30] British belief in the beneficent effects of competitive struggle had not yet succumbed to the ethos of the welfare state.

It should be apparent from the foregoing discussion that there was nothing original in Darwin's views on social evolution except the general perspective provided by his theory of evolution by natural selection, and that had been anticipated to a considerable degree in the matter of social evolution by Herbert Spencer's writings in the 1850s. Darwin did little, if any, original research on social evolution, but he read widely in search of information that would illustrate the applicability of his theory of natural selection to the case of man. Before 1859, as we have seen, his attention was focused on the struggle for existence among tribes and races in early human history, with special emphasis on races as the human equivalent of the varieties produced by natural selection among animals generally. But he decided to omit this aspect of his theory from the *Origin of Species* in order not to distract attention from the main theme.

The publication of Darwin's *Origin of Species* led inevitably to attempts, especially in Britain, to apply the theory of natural selection to the favorite problem of nineteenth-century social theorists: the causes of progress and retrogression in human history. Building on the tradition of British political economy, Spencer had already stressed the importance of competitive struggle and survival of the fittest, aided by the inherited effects of mental and moral exercise, in social evolution; and Bagehot, Galton, and others soon followed suit in the wake of Darwin's *Origin of Species*. In less than a decade the idea of progress through competitive struggle was elevated from the status of a principle of political economy to that of a law governing biological and social evolution. The "Lamarckian" principle of the inheritance of acquired characters, far from constituting a rival principle of explanation, was viewed as cooperating with the law of natural selection in bringing about the gradual improvement of the human race. Finally, the sense of Western, and more especially British or Anglo-Saxon, superiority over other nations and races seemed confirmed by the findings of science as well as by the progress of history.

There can be little doubt that Darwin shared these ebullient beliefs in the upward progress of mankind through the competition of individuals, tribes, nations, and races and the inherited effects of mental and moral exercise, in the peculiar excellence of the Anglo-Saxon people, and in the gradual triumph of superior races over those "lower in the scale." In November 1878, he confided to G. A. Gaskell his reservations about artificial checks on human procreation:

> Suppose that such checks had been in action during the last two or three centuries, or even for a shorter time in Britain, what a difference it would have made in the world, when we consider America, Australia, New Zealand, and S. Africa. No words can exaggerate the importance, in my opinion, of our colonisation for the future history of the world.
>
> If it were universally known that the birth of children could be prevented, and this were not thought immoral by married persons, would there not be great danger of extreme profligacy amongst unmarried women, and might we not become like the "arreoi" societies in the Pacific? In the course of a century France will tell us the result in many ways, and we can already see that the French nation does not spread or increase much.[31]

Again, in 1881, less than a year before his death, Darwin reaffirmed his faith in the efficacy of natural selection in human history in a letter to William Graham:

> I could show fight on natural selection having done and doing more for the progress of civilization than you seem inclined to admit. Remember what risk the nations of Europe ran, not so many centuries ago, of being overwhelmed by the Turks, and how ridiculous such an idea now is! The more civilized so-called Caucasian races have beaten the Turkish hollow in the struggle for existence. Looking to the world at no very distant date, what an endless number of the lower races will have been eliminated by the higher civilized races throughout the world.[32]

This view of history would find few supporters today, but we should not therefore rush to brand Darwin a "racist" or dismiss him as a bourgeois exponent of British imperialism. If, as seems clear, he shared the belief of most of his contemporaries in the existence of racial differences in intellectual ability and moral disposition, he did so because he thought the evidence seemed to require it, and he qualified his statements in cases where the evidence seemed contradictory, as in the case of the moral differences "believed to exist" between human races. Ever the cautious scientist, Darwin was much more reserved and open-minded in his judgments on the heritability of acquired characters, the superior talents of the Anglo-Saxon peoples, and the role of natural selection in history than were most of the writers whose works he read and annotated. Above all, he was careful to recognize "the obligations of enlightened humanity" toward the peoples of every nation and race and to make it clear that, whatever the deleterious genetic effects of preserving the sick, the weak, and the imbecile, people must obey the promptings of their sympathetic impulses, for these, too, were products of the evolutionary process. But even with respect to these impulses of our "nobler nature," Darwin could not resist hoping that they, too, would eventually become part of man's genetic endowment, "fixed by inheritance." Only if nurture could be transformed into nature by natural selection and the inherited effects of habit and moral training could Darwin enjoy the high satisfaction of believing that he and Lyell and Huxley—yes, even Shakespeare and Newton—would some day be looked back on as mere savages by a remote posterity shaped to a higher destiny by the patient processes of nature-history.

From the foregoing account of the development of Darwin's ideas about social evolution it seems fair to conclude that what we call "social Darwinism"—the belief that competition between individuals, tribes, nations, and races has been an important, if not the chief, engine of progress in human history—was endemic in much of British thought in the mid-nineteenth century, that Darwin's *Origin of Species* gave a powerful boost to this kind of thinking, and that Darwin himself was deeply influenced by this current of thought. We should not jump to the conclusion that all British social thought was of this character, however. As John W. Burrow has shown in his excellent book *Evolution and Society: A Study in Victorian Social Theory*, Sir Henry Maine, J. F. McLennan, Edward Tylor, John Stuart Mill, and others made important contributions to social theory without benefit of Spencerian or Darwinian ideas.[33] Nevertheless, it is clear that more attention should be paid to the intellectual milieu in which Darwin worked. The idea that Darwin, unlike Spencer and other contemporaries, was a pure scientist confronting nature unhampered by preconceived ideas about nature, society, man, and God must be abandoned. Like every other scientist, Darwin approached nature, human nature, and society with ideas derived from his culture, however much his scientific researches may have changed those ideas in the long run. This essay has given some idea of the assumptions about man and society he imbibed from British culture along with Spencer, Wallace, Bagehot, Galton, and Greg. The next essay will attempt to delineate a more general Spencerian-Darwinian world view on which Spencer, Darwin, Wallace, and Huxley converged about 1860, only to diverge again before the century had run its course.

NOTES

1. Marvin Harris, *The Rise of Anthropological Theory: A History of Theories of Culture* (New York: Thomas Y. Crowell Co., 1968), pp. 116–123.

2. Derek Freeman, "The Evolutionary Theories of Charles Darwin and Herbert Spencer," *Current Anthropology*, 15 (1974): 221. Fifteen commentaries and a reply by Freeman follow this essay.

3. Robert Young, "Malthus and the Evolutionists: The Common Context of Biological and Social Theory," *Past and Present*, 1969, pp. 109–145, stresses the Malthusian context of the writings of Spencer, Darwin, Wallace, and others. Gertrude Himmelfarb, *Darwin and the Darwinian Revolution* (Garden City, N.Y.: Doubleday, 1959), chap. 19, takes the position that Darwin was not interested in the bearing of his theory on problems of social evolution. John S. Haller, Jr., *Outcasts from Evolution: Scientific Attitudes of Racial Inferiority, 1859–1900* (Urbana: University of Illinois Press, 1971), pp. 86–88, recognizes that Darwin believed in the existence of superior and inferior races but does not discuss his social evolutionism. Richard Hofstadter, *Social Darwinism in American Thought*, rev. ed. (Boston: Beacon Press, 1955), pp. 90–91, seems uncertain whether to regard Darwin as a "social Darwinist" or not, stressing the contradictory character of his utterances in this connection. Jacob W. Gruber, "Darwinism and Its Critics," *Hist. Sci.*, 3 (1964):

123, states that "Darwin did not use the idea of competition or 'struggle for existence' in the interpersonal and aggressive sense in which Spencer and the social Darwinists used it." Howard E. Gruber, in H. E. Gruber and Paul H. Barrett, *Darwin on Man: A Psychological Study of Scientific Creativity* (New York: E. P. Dutton, 1974), p. 240, asserts that Darwin "never entertained" the social Darwinist idea of "the pitiless struggle of man against man as a defensible social arrangement." The foregoing are but a few of the varying and contradictory opinions concerning Darwin's views as a social evolutionist.

4. Charles Darwin, *The Descent of Man and Selection in Relation to Sex* (New York: D. Appleton, 1896), p. 618.

5. Thomas F. Glick, ed., *The Comparative Reception of Darwinism* (Austin: University of Texas Press, 1972).

6. Darwin to Charles Lyell, Ilkley, Yorkshire, 11 October 1859, quoted in *The Life and Letters of Charles Darwin*, ed. Francis Darwin, 3 vols. (London: John Murray, 1888), 2: 211. See also in the same volume, p. 334, Darwin's comment in a letter to Lyell 23 September 1860): "The white man is 'improving off the face of the earth' even races nearly his equals."

7. As transcribed from Darwin's Notebook E in Gruber and Barrett, *Darwin on Man*, p. 459.

8. For some reason Darwin drew a line through "New Zealanders" in this annotation. He also underlined the words "the weeds" in Wallace's account of how the superior physical, moral, and intellectual qualities of the European enabled him to increase at the expense of savage man, "just as the weeds of Europe overrun North America and Australia, extinguishing native productions by the inherent vigour of their organisation, and by their greater capacity for existence and multiplication." See A. R. Wallace, "The Origin of Human Races and the Antiquity of Man Deduced from the Theory of 'Natural Selection,' " *Anthropological Review* 2 (1864), clxv.

9. Darwin to A. R. Wallace, Down, Bromley, Kent, 28 May 1864, quoted in *Alfred Russel Wallace: Letters and Reminiscences*, ed. James Marchant, 2 vols. (New York: Harper and Brothers, 1916), 2: 127. See also Darwin to Wallace, 26 January 1870, ibid., pp. 205–206.

10. Charles Darwin, *The Variation of Animals and Plants under Domestication*, 2 vols. (London: John Murray, 1868), 2: 7.

11. Francis Galton, "Hereditary Talent and Character," part 1, *Macmillan's Magazine*, 12 (June 1865): 166.

12. Darwin, *Descent of Man*, p. 134.

13. William R. Greg, "On the Failure of 'Natural Selection' in the Case of Man," *Fraser's Magazine for Town and Country*, September 1868, p. 356.

14. Francis Galton to Charles Darwin, 42 Nutland Gate S.W., 28 January 1870 (item 160, vol. 80, Darwin Correspondence, Cambridge University Library).

15. Walter Bagehot, "Physics and Politics," *The Fortnightly Review*, April 1, 1868, p. 456.

16. Ibid., p. 467.

17. Darwin, *Variation of Animals and Plants*, 2: 46–47.

18. Charles Darwin, *More Letters of Charles Darwin*, ed. Francis Darwin, 2 vols. (London: John Murray, 1903), 1: 298.

19. David Page, *Man: Where, Whence and Whither. Being a Glance at Man in His Natural-History Relations* (Edinburgh: Edmonston and Douglas, 1867), p. 91.

20. Charles Darwin to Charles Lyell, Down, 27 April 1860, quoted in *More Letters* vol. 2: 30: "I cannot explain why, but to me it would be an infinite satisfaction to believe that mankind will progress to such a pitch that we should [look] back at [ourselves] as mere Barbarians." See also the quotation in n. 3 and Darwin to Lyell dated 4 January 1860 *Life and Letters*, 2: 262.

21. Page, *Man: Where, Whence and Whither*, p. 92.

22. Darwin, *Descent of Man*, p. 128.

23. Ibid., p. 129.

24. Ibid., p. 130.

25. Ibid., p. 132.

26. Ibid., pp. 123–124.

27. Ibid., p. 124.

28. Ibid., p. 140.

29. Ibid., p. 143.

30. Ibid., p. 618.

31. Darwin to G. A. Gaskell, Down, 15 November 1878, quoted in *More Letters*, 2: 50.

32. Darwin to William Graham, Down, 3 July 1881, quoted in *Life and Letters*, 1: 316.

33. John W. Burrow, *Evolution and Society: A Study in Victorian Social Theory* (Cambridge: Cambridge University Press, 1966).

SUGGESTED FURTHER READING

There is a large literature on "social Darwinism," much of it controversial. Derek Freeman's article "The Evolutionary Theories of Charles Darwin and Herbert Spencer," cited in the present essay, is an extended critique of Marvin Harris's conflation of the views of Darwin and Spencer under the rubric of "biological Spencerism" in his *The Rise of Anthropological Theory* (London: Routledge and Kegan Paul, 1968). Appended to Freeman's essay are a useful bibliography and commentaries by various authors. See also John C. Greene, *Darwin and the Modern World View* (Baton Rouge: Louisiana State University Press, 1961), chap. 3; J. W. Burrow, *Evolution and Society: A Study in Victorian Social Theory* (Cambridge: Cambridge University Press, 1966); Kenneth E. Bock, "Darwin and Social Theory," *Philosophy of Science* 22 (1955): 123–134; Robert Young, "Darwin's Metaphor: Does Nature Select?" *Monist* 55 (1971): 442–503; Barry G. Gale, "Darwin and the Concept of the Struggle for Existence," *Isis* 63 (1972): 321–344; Peter J. Bowler, "Malthus, Darwin, and the Concept of Struggle," *Journal of the History of Ideas* 37 (1976): 631–650; James Rogers, "Darwinism and Social Darwinism," ibid., 30 (1972): 265–280.

For Wallace's views, see Roger Smith, "A. R. Wallace: Philosophy of Nature and Man," *British Journal of the History of Science* 6 (1972): 177–199; Malcolm J. Kottler, "Alfred R. Wallace, the Origin of Man, and Spiritualism," *Isis* 65 (1974): 145–192; Frank Miller Turner, *Between Science and Religion: The Reaction to Scientific Naturalism in Late Victorian England* (New Haven and London: Yale University Press, 1974), chap. 4; Wilma George, *Biologist Philosopher: A Study of the Life and Writings of Alfred Russel Wallace* (London: Abelard-Schuman, 1964).

6

DARWINISM AS A WORLD VIEW

Isms are the stock in trade of scholars who study the history of ideas. But, although their discourse is full of isms—Marxism, Cartesianism, Newtonianism, Freudianism, Spencerianism, Darwinism, and the like—they have no established rules for defining them. Everyone uses these terms as seems best, defining them as precisely or loosely (if at all) as the occasion or the argument seems to demand.

Among the various isms, none has been defined with less precision than Darwinism. In his book *Darwinism Comes to America*, George Daniels tells the reader that Darwinism is simply Darwin's theory of organic evolution through random variation, struggle for existence, and natural selection. This seems a limited definition (Daniels does not stick to it, nor do the nineteenth-century authors whom he anthologizes), and it runs counter to the habitual practice of intellectual historians of distinguishing between scientific theories and the general views of reality extrapolated from them. Few scholars would define Newtonianism as Newton's three laws of motion and the law of universal gravitation or Freudianism as Freud's theory of neurotic behavior.

Other scholars equate Darwinism with evolution, but this usage is unfair to Lamarck, Robert Chambers, and other early evolutionists, to say nothing of the confusion it introduces into intellectual history by concealing the great differences that distinguish various types of evolutionism from each other. Still other writers, seeking to emphasize these distinctions, contrast Darwinism as a scientific theory with Lamarckianism, stressing the reliance of Lamarck, Spencer, and others on the inheritance of acquired characters in contrast to Darwin's habitual emphasis on natural selection of congenital traits.

128

Unfortunately, Darwin believed to a considerable extent in the inheritance of acquired characters and assigned this mode of modification an important, though subsidiary, role in organic evolution in the *Origin of Species* and an even more important role in *The Descent of Man* and *The Expression of Emotions in Man and Animals.*

Still others define Darwinism as a philosophy of science, contrasting Darwin's scientific caution and continual effort to verify his hypotheses by observation and experiment with the high-flown speculative methods of men like Herbert Spencer. Doubtless Darwin was a scientist par excellence, hesitant about pushing his conclusions farther than the evidence seemed to warrant. But he could be as speculative as Spencer in hypothesizing about the origin and development of man's distinctively human attributes, drawing heavily on the speculations of Spencer himself—"our great philosopher"—in his theorizing on these subjects. In any case, since Darwin was by his own declaration no philosopher, it seems a little quixotic to define Darwinism as Darwin's philosophy of science.

Next, there is "social Darwinism," generally understood to refer to the view that human progress is the outcome of competitive struggle among individuals, tribes, nations, and races. As we shall see, Darwin expressed views of this kind frequently, especially in *The Descent of Man,* but the same view had been advocated well before 1859 by Robert Knox, Herbert Spencer, and others.

Finally—if one can really reach an end of definitions of Darwinism—there are those who use the term Darwinism to refer to an all-embracing view of reality—nature, man, society, history, science, and so forth—which they believe to be implicit, if not always explicit, in Darwin's writings. Sometimes these wider views are referred to as the "implications" of Darwinism. Unfortunately for this view of things, Darwin himself never elaborated a general view of reality, and his commentators have not been explicit in spelling out these "implications" of Darwinism except with reference to particular issues that interest them. There is the additional difficulty that many of the general views about reality implicit in Darwin's writings were not peculiar to him but may be found expressed more clearly and succinctly in the writings of his contemporaries, notably Herbert Spencer and T. H. Huxley.

My own view of these difficulties and ambiguities is that the suffix *ism* should be reserved for general views of reality (natural or social) connected with scientific theories instead of being used to denote the theories themselves, and that the word *Darwinism* should be used to designate a world view that seems to have been arrived at more or less independently by Spencer, Darwin, Huxley, and Wallace in the late 1850s and early 1860s, although this convergence of opinion began to display signs of divergence soon afterward. The purpose of this paper will be to attempt to delineate the world view on which these four men converged about the time of publication of Darwin's *Origin of Species*, first by enumerating and discussing the various currents of Western thought that came together to form what I call Darwinism and, second, by illustrating briefly the way in which these currents were blended in the thought of each of the four men.

The oldest and most general component of the world view that came to be known as Darwinism was the idea of nature as a law-bound system of matter in motion, the mechanical view of nature (with its corollary of primary and secondary qualities) elaborated in the seventeenth century by Galileo, Descartes, Boyle, Newton, and others. To speculative thinkers like Descartes this mechanistic cosmology opened up the exhilarating prospect of deriving the present structures of nature—stars, solar systems, and others—from a previous, more homogeneous state of the universal system of matter in motion by the operation of the laws of nature. "Give me extension and movement and I will remake the world," said Descartes. Newton, Boyle, and John Ray were horrified at the idea of "feigning hypotheses" to explain all things mechanically by "a slight hypothesis of matter so and so divided and mov'd." To them it seemed evident and proper that the same God who had created the particles of matter and set them in motion should have arranged their motions from the beginning so that they would produce the harmonious system of mutually adapted structures constituting the present order of nature.

But it was to the Cartesian rather than to the Newtonian view of the law-bound system of matter in motion that the future belonged. The speculative temptation to derive the present structures of nature from previous states of the system of nature by the operation of natural laws was too strong to be resisted. In the next century and a half it gave rise to the cosmic evolutionism of Kant and Herschel, to the Kant-La Place nebular hypothesis, to Buffon's theory of the origin of the solar system, to the geological uniformitarianism of Hutton and Lyell, to Buffon's transformist ideas and the full-blown evolutionism of Erasmus Darwin and Lamarck.

In the writings of Erasmus Darwin and Lamarck, Western thought adumbrated the second component of what was to be known as Darwinism: the idea of organic evolution from the simplest to the most complex living forms, including man, through the operations of the system of nature. Both Erasmus Darwin and Lamarck regarded this system of nature as having been established by a wise and beneficent deity in such a way as to ensure perpetual and indefinite improvement in the organic realm. The progress in the organic world, said Erasmus Darwin, was "analogous to the improving excellence observable in every part of the creation; such as in the progressive increase of the solid or habitable parts of the earth from water; and in the progressive increase of the wisdom and happiness of its inhabitants." To Lamarck, man was simply the latest and thus far the highest of nature's productions, an animal whose brain and nervous system had been evolved from that of an ape by natural processes that were continually generating simple organisms from inorganic matter and perfecting them with the aid of "plenty of time and circumstances" in accordance with laws ordained by "the sublime Author of Nature."

About the same time that Erasmus Darwin and Lamarck were concocting the second ingredient of what was later to be called Darwinism, a third ingredient was being prepared by Adam Smith, Thomas Malthus, and David Ricardo. These founders of the British school of political economy championed the idea that free competition in the marketplace was a divinely ordained system of natural liberty that, if allowed to operate by its own laws of supply and demand, would produce, as if by the guidance of a divine hand, the wealth of nations and the progress of mankind. In its early, optimistic phase the emphasis of British political economy was on the necessarily beneficent outcome of free competition. In the writings of Malthus and Ricardo, however, the dark side of the doctrine became apparent. Since mankind tended to multiply incontinently at a geometric rate and the food supply could increase at no more than an arithmetic rate, population must always tend to outrun the food supply, increasing the amount of labor available and driving wages down until such time as famine, disease, vice, and poverty should reduce the supply of labor though the vicissitudes of the struggle for existence.

This competitive ethos was to exert a powerful influence on the thinking of Darwin, Wallace, and Spencer when combined with the idea of organic evolution and with another idea emerging among social theorists on the Continent: the idea of a science of human progress based on laws analogous to those governing the physical world. Adumbrated in the writings of Rousseau, Turgot, and Condorcet, this concept was clearly articulated in Auguste Comte's project of a social physics—or sociology, as he later called it—which would discover the laws and stages of historical development and show "by what necessary chain of successive transformations the human race, starting from a condition barely superior to that of a society of great apes, has been gradually led up to the present stage of European civilization." Comte's reference to the great apes implied no belief on his part in the idea of organic evolution. Like most other social theorists of his day he rejected Lamarck's development hypothesis and regarded man's capacity to undergo evolution in his nature and institutions as a characteristic that distinguished him from animals. It was not until the idea of social evolution was linked to the idea of organic evolution in the middle of the century that the concept of nature-history as a single continuum undergoing progressive development emerged as the central theme of evolutionary naturalism.

A final ingredient in the world view that came to be called Darwinism was the stream of Lockean epistemology and sensationalist psychology that ran strong in the English-speaking world and taught all whom it influenced to reject notions of innate ideas, intuition, and the like and to rely upon sense experience as the source of all knowledge. In the nineteenth century this intellectual tendency was powerfully reinforced and given new expression by a growing positivistic faith in the methods of natural science as man's sole means of gaining knowledge of reality. Since science was increasingly conceived as the search for the laws governing the phenomena presented in sense experience, the hope of discovering or knowing a reality behind the veil of sense experience diminished as the prestige of science grew. Positivism led to agnosticism.

Thus, by the middle of the nineteenth century all of the materials that were to be forged into a distinctive kind of evolutionary world view lay at hand—the law-bound system of matter in motion, evolutionary deism verging toward agnosticism under the influence of positivistic empiricism, the idea of organic evolution, the idea of a social science of historical development, faith in the beneficent effects of competitive struggle—all these ideas lay waiting for the architect who could combine them into a single all-embracing synthesis. That architect was Herbert Spencer. As a self-educated engineer, Spencer was familiar with the principles of mechanics and the wider mechanistic cosmology associated with them since the seventeenth century, as well as with further developments in physical science in the nineteenth century leading to the enunication of the principle of the conservation of energy. He early accepted the nebular hypothesis of Kant and Laplace and continued to defend it in his writings. About 1840, on reading Lyell's refutation of Lamarck's evolutionary theory, he adopted the idea of organic evolution. He was also familiar with the theories of Comte and other social evolutionists and with the laissez-faire doctrines of Smith, Malthus, and Bentham, the latter of which he adopted as his own. He had read also William Carpenter's exposition of Karl Ernst von Baer's embryological ideas and Robert Chambers's *Vestiges of the Natural History of Creation,* where for the first time the nebular hypothesis, geological uniformitarianism, organic evolution and some degree of social evolutionism were combined within a framework of evolutionary deism.

In the 1850s, beginning with his book *Social Statics,* Spencer gradually sketched the outlines of a comprehensive evolutionary philosophy incorporating all of the fundamental ideas indicated above and subsuming them under the general idea of "progress," which he defined as a constant passage from homogeneity to heterogeneity owing to the principle that every cause has more than one effect. By means of this principle he was able to interpret all phenomena—cosmic, geological, organic, social, linguistic, and so forth—in terms of "the redistribution of matter and motion." "Progress," he declared in 1857, "is not an accident, not a thing within human control, but a beneficent necessity." Here with a vengeance was the law-bound system of matter in motion, extended now to embrace organic nature, human history, and society. The adjective *beneficent,* with which Spencer qualified the necessity inherent in this universal system, was a vestige of the evolutionary deism that had informed his *Social Statics;* the word *progress* was a reflection of his overriding concern with social philosophy. By the time of his *First Principles* (1861), however, Spencer had substituted the Unknowable for his earlier deistic Creator and replaced the term *progress* with the less anthropocentric term *evolution,* defined as "an integration of matter and concomitant dissipation of motion; during which the matter passes from an indefinite, incoherent homogeneity to a definite, coherent heterogeneity; and during which the retained motion undergoes a parallel transformation."

In his theory of social evolution Spencer was a "Darwinian" before Darwin, emphasizing the efficacy of population pressure, the struggle for existence, and survival of the fittest among individuals, tribes, nations, and races as the primary engine of advancement in mankind's slow progress from its early bestial condition, in which men were governed by force, fear, and hero worship, to its eventual state, in which government would wither away because all men would possess by nature an instinctive regard for the rights of others as well as for their own rights. In his organic evolutionism, however, Spencer relied primarily on evolutionary modification through use and disuse and various environmental influences, assuming the heritability of acquired characteristics. After Darwin published his *Origin of Species*, Spencer continued to urge the importance of use-modification as an evolutionary agency, but he also took advantage of the opportunity Darwin presented him to subsume both social and organic evolution under the principle of the struggle for existence and the survival of the fittest.

It will be apparent from the foregoing discussion that Spencerianism was a clearly articulated and comprehensive view of reality of which the leading ingredients were: (1) a unitary conception of nature-history as a law-bound system of matter in motion undergoing continual progress or evolution from homogeneity toward heterogeneity, (2) evolutionary deism eventuating in agnosticism under the influence of positivistic conceptions of the sources of human knowledge, (3) a naturalistic conception of man and human history as the latest productions of the system of nature, (4) belief in competitive struggle and the inheritance of functionally and environmentally produced modifications as the chief mechanisms of progress in organic and social evolution, (5) positivistic faith in the methods of natural science as man's chief reliance in attaining knowledge of reality.

To what extent were these essentials of the Spencerian world view accepted and shared by Darwin? Unfortunately for the intellectual historian, Darwin never undertook to expound his world view systematically. A scientist rather than a philosopher, he distrusted Spencer's wide-ranging speculative approach to reality and confined himself to constructing scientific theories on the basis of laborious research. To Darwin, Spencer's effort to conceive all the phenomena of the universe as a single continuum governed by a single evolutionary law must have seemed overambitious, highly speculative, and incapable of scientific verification. At the same time it is apparent from his reference to Spencer as "our great philosopher" and from his tribute to Spencer's pioneering work in helping to develop a naturalistic psychology on evolutionary assumptions as well as from his comments on Spencer's ideas in *The Descent of Man* and *The Expression of Emotion in Man and Animals* that he respected Spencer and admired (perhaps even envied) his speculative virtuosity. Moreover, a close reading of Darwin's writings, including his correspondence, shows that although he regarded Spencer's "synthetic philosophy" as overambitious and incapable of scientific verification, he nevertheless held views of nature, man, God, history, and social progress that were remarkably like those of Spencer and derived from similar sources.

In Darwin's *Origin of Species* we find expressed the same mechanistic evolutionary deism and evolutionized natural theology that characterized Spencer's early writings. In the next to the last paragraph of the *Origin of Species* Darwin declared his conviction that "it accords better with what we know of the laws impressed on matter by the Creator, that the production and extinction of the past and present inhabitants of the world have been due to secondary causes, like those determining the birth and death of the individual." In the same paragraph Darwin echoed Spencer's faith that this system of secondary causes was inherently progressive when he declared that "as natural selection works solely by and for the good of each being, all corporeal and mental endowments will tend to progress towards perfection." Indeed, the *Origin* teems with references to the "improvements" brought about in nature by the operation of natural selection. Chapter 4 ends with Paleyesque reflections on the brighter side of the dark struggle for existence: "When we reflect on this struggle, we may console ourselves with the full belief, that the war of nature is not incessant, that no fear is felt, that death is generally prompt, and the vigorous, the healthy, and the happy survive and multiply."

That Darwin conceived the beneficent effects of competition and natural selection as extending to the human as well as the organic world is apparent from his letters to Lyell in 1859, in which he argued that improvement is built into the evolutionary process.

> When you contrast natural selection and "improvement," you seem always to overlook . . . that every step in the natural selection of each species implies improvement in that species in relation to its conditions of life. . . . Improvement implies, I suppose, each form obtaining many parts or organs, all excellently adapted for their functions. As each species is improved, and as the number of forms will have increased, if we look to the whole course of time, the organic condition of life for other forms will become more complex, and there will be a necessity for other forms to become improved, or they will be exterminated: and I can see no limit to this process of improvement, without the intervention of any other and direct principle of improvement. All this seems to me quite compatible with certain forms fitted for simple conditions, remaining unaltered, or being degraded.
>   If I have a second edition, I will reiterate "Natural Selection," and, as a general consequence, Natural Improvement.[1]

Again:

> I suppose you do not doubt that the intellectual powers are as important for the welfare of each being as corporeal structures; if so, I can see no difficulty in the most intellectual individuals of a species being continually selected; and the intellect of the new species thus improved, aided probably by effects of inherited mental exercise. I look at this process as now going on with the races of man; the less intellectual races being exterminated.[2]

Spencer himself could scarcely have given better expression to the idea that competitive struggle and survival of the fittest, aided by use-inheritance, generate progress in nature-history by a kind of "beneficent necessity," as Spencer had called it in 1857. For Spencer, the Creator God who had established this system of improving beneficence in nature-history had faded into a remote Unknowable by 1861. Darwin was still a deist in 1859, but the same inner logic that had converted Spencer's evolutionary deism into agnosticism was to work a similar change in Darwin's views by the time he published *The Descent of Man*. Even in 1860 his deistic faith was riddled with doubts, as he confessed to Asa Gray:

> I had no intention to write atheistically. But I own that I cannot
> see as plainly as others do, and as I should wish to do, evidence
> of design and beneficence on all sides of us. There seems to me
> too much misery in the world. . . . On the other hand, I cannot
> anyhow be contented to view this wonderful universe, and
> especially the nature of man, and to conclude that everything is
> the result of brute force. I am inclined to look at everything as
> resulting from designed laws, with the details, whether good or
> bad, left to the working out of what we may call chance.[3]

By the time of *The Descent of Man* the deistic underpinning of Darwin's belief in progress in nature-history had been largely eroded. But the belief in a law-bound system of nature-history and in the progressive tendency of the operations of that system remained. If anything, Darwin was more rather than less Spencerian in his views than he had been in 1859, if only because he had now to deal with the evolution of human nature and society, subjects on which Spencer had been writing since 1850. Like Spencer, Darwin presented man as a product of evolutionary processes operating according to fixed laws, but whereas Spencer had placed his main reliance on environmentally and functionally induced modifications as the mechanism of evolutionary change, Darwin relied mainly on natural selection in the struggle for existence, supplemented by sexual selection and by use-inheritance.

When he came to explain the origin of man's distinctively human attributes and the causes of progress and retrogression in human society, Darwin drew on Spencer in a double sense. On the one hand, he echoed Spencer in his insistence on the importance of competitive struggle among individuals, tribes, nations, and races as a force for improvement in human society and civilization. The passages to this effect in *The Descent of Man* are too familiar to require quoting at length. Perhaps the most dramatic is the one in which Darwin contrasts the "vigorous state of health" enjoyed by savages subject to the beneficial pruning of natural selection with the debilitated condition of civilized peoples, among whom hospitals, asylums, poor laws, and medical science enable the imbecile, the sick, and other mentally or physically deficient persons to propagate their kind. "No one," concludes Darwin, "who has attended to the breeding of domestic animals will doubt that this must be highly injurious to the race of man." Less dramatic but more revealing of Darwin's debt to Adam Smith and Thomas Malthus is his declaration in the "General Summary" to the work that men would "sink into indolence" and cease to progress if the struggle for existence that had brought mankind to its present high condition were greatly diminished.

Equally reminiscent of Spencer is Darwin's speculative account of the origin and development of man's moral sense from his social instincts through the action of natural selection and use-inheritance. Man's social instincts, he speculated, must have developed out of parental and filial affections "to a large extent through natural selection." Once acquired, these social instincts would possess survival value and would be strengthened by habit as well as by natural selection. From this point on, wrote Darwin, primitive man "would from an inherited tendency be willing to defend, in concert with others, his fellow men; and would be ready to aid them in any way, which did not too greatly interfere with his own welfare or his own strong desires." Out of the conflict between personal desires and the social instincts conscience would be born, accompanied by feelings of guilt and shame, and would develop through habit and natural selection.

> Man prompted by his conscience, will through long habit acquire such perfect self-command, that his desires and passions will at last yield instantly and without a struggle to his social sympathies and instincts, including his feeling for the judgment of his fellows. . . . It is possible . . . even probable, that the habit of self-command may, like other habits, be inherited.[4]

At this point in his argument, Darwin quoted Spencer's dictum that "the experiences of the human race have been producing corresponding modifications which, by continued transmission and accumulation, have become in us certain faculties of moral intuition . . . which have no apparent basis in the individual experiences of utility" and expressed his own hope "that virtuous habits will grow stronger, becoming perhaps fixed by inheritance."

It appears, then, that the general views concerning nature, man, God, society, and history that can be gleaned from Darwin's writings are remarkably similar to those underlying Herbert Spencer's more systematic philosophy. Both men inherited from the seventeenth century the concept of nature as a law-bound system of matter in motion and attempted to expand it to embrace organic and human evolution. Both regarded social evolution as continuous with organic evolution and as governed in its progressive development by the same laws and processes, notably natural selection and the inherited effects of habit, use, and disuse. In his theory of organic evolution Darwin laid relatively more emphasis on natural selection than Spencer did and less on environmentally and functionally induced modifications, though both men acknowledged the operation of all these factors. In their theories of social evolution both men viewed human progress as the result primarily of a gradual improvement in the intellectual and instinctual endowment of the human race, brought about partly by competitive struggle among individuals, tribes, nations, and races and partly by the inherited effects of habit and training. Reared in Christian environments, both men became evolutionary deists and eventually agnostics. Both were powerfully influenced by the positivistic faith of the nineteenth century in science as the sovereign key to knowledge of reality. Spencer cannot justly be called Darwinian, since his evolutionary philosophy had been worked out in all its essentials before Darwin published his *Origin of Species*, and it retained those essential features despite some adjustments required to take account of Darwin's publications. Darwin, on the contrary, may justly be called a Spencerian in his general view of nature, man, God, history, and society, even though he never adopted Spencer's synthetic philosophy *in toto*, distrusted Spencer's intellectual methods, emphasized natural selection more than use-inheritance as the mechanism of organic evolution, and was less consistent than Spencer in embracing competitive struggle as an engine of social progress.

If Herbert Spencer first outlined the evolutionary world view that also informed Darwin's writings, it was Thomas Henry Huxley who became the chief expounder and champion of Darwinism after the publication of the *Origin of Species*. To delineate Huxley's concept of Darwinism is not easy, since his views changed with the passage of time and his utterances before scientific audiences sometimes diverged from those set forth in his popular essays and speeches. An examination of his writings in the 1860s shows, however, that his views of nature, man, God, science, history, and society at this time were strikingly similar to those we have attributed to Darwin and Spencer.

In his acceptance of the mechanistic cosmology of the seventeenth century and its relevance for nineteenth-century evolutionism, Huxley was as explicit as any intellectual historian could wish. In an essay entitled "Evolution in Biology" he laid it down as "the fundamental proposition of Evolution" (note the capital *E*) that "the whole world, living and not living, is the result of the mutual interaction, according to definite laws, of the forces possessed by the molecules of which the primitive nebulosity of the universe was composed" and went on to declare that this view was held in all its essentials by René Descartes, the spirit of whose *Principles of Philosophy* had been revived, said Huxley, in "the profound and vigourous writings of Mr. Spencer."[5]

These passages display in the clearest light the historical connection between Descartes's mechanistic vortex theory, the nebular hypothesis of Kant, Laplace, and Herschel, and the universal evolutionism of Herbert Spencer. Other passages from Huxley's writings in this period exhibit the same transition from evolutionary deism and Christian providentialism to blind agnosticism that one encounters in Darwin's and Spencer's writings. Thus, in 1860, in an essay entitled "The Origin of Species," Huxley undertook to depict "the picture which science draws of the world":

> Harmonious order governing eternally continuous progress—the web and woof of matter and force interweaving by slow degrees, without a broken thread, that veil which lies between us and the Infinite—the universe which alone we know or can know; such is the picture which science draws of the world, and in proportion as any part of that picture is in unison with the rest, so may we feel sure that it is rightly painted.[6]

Except for their literary quality, these words might as well have been penned by Spencer as by Huxley.

Huxley's reference to "eternally continuous progress" resulting from the harmoniously ordered operations of matter and force shows that, despite his insistence from time to time that evolution was not necessarily progressive, he shared the faith of Darwin and Spencer in "Nature's great progression, from the formless to the formed—from the inorganic to the organic—from blind force to conscious intellect and will," as he himself expressed it. That natural selection was the primary cause of this progression in the organic world Huxley had no doubt. As to the role of competitive struggle and survival of the fittest in human society and history, however, Huxley's views underwent a striking change. In his essay "A Liberal Education," published in 1868, Huxley evinced a Spencerian delight in the struggle for existence, likening human life to a chess game played according to rules laid down by a Master Chess Player whose play is always "fair, just, and patient" but who "never overlooks a mistake, or makes the smallest allowance for ignorance," checkmating "without haste, but without remorse" those who play badly. Then, with a sudden change of metaphors, the universe becomes "Nature's university," in which all mankind are enrolled.

> Those who take honors in Nature's university [Huxley writes], who learn the laws which govern men and things and obey them, are the really great and successful men in this world. The great mass of mankind are the "Poll," who pick up just enough to get through without much discredit. Those who won't learn at

all are plucked; and then you can't come up again. Nature's pluck means extermination.[7]

The liberally educated man, Huxley concludes, is he who has learned to live in harmony with Nature. "They will get on together rarely; she as his ever beneficent mother; he as her mouth-piece, her conscious self, her minister and interpreter." A far cry this from the Huxley of the Romanes lecture (1893), to whom it seemed evident that "the ethical progress of society depends not on imitating the cosmic process, still less in running away from it, but in combating it."

In Huxley's early writings, too, we find a clear expression of the positivistic faith in scientific method as the sovereign key to reliable knowledge of reality which characterized Spencer and Darwin. This faith, with its accompanying overtones of agnosticism and belief in progress through the ever wider extension of scientific method, was set forth unambiguously in Huxley's essay "On the Advisableness of Improving Natural Knowledge", published in 1866. After rebuking those who saw nothing more in science than a means of increasing human comfort and enjoyment, he went on to proclaim that "natural knowledge, seeking to satisfy natural wants, has found the ideas which can alone still spiritual cravings" and that "natural knowledge, in desiring to ascertain the laws of comfort, has been driven to discover those of conduct, and to lay the foundations of a new morality." "The man of science," he declared, "has learned to believe in justification, not by faith, but by verification." Looking to the future, when science should have remodeled the intellectual ethics of mankind, Huxley envisaged a "New Reformation":

> If these ideas be destined, as I believe they are, to be more and more firmly established as the world grows older; if that spirit [the ethical spirit inculcated by science] be fated, as I believe it is, to extend itself into all departments of human thought, and to become co-extensive with the range of knowledge; if, as our race approaches its maturity, it discovers, as I believe it will, that there is but one kind of knowledge and but one method of acquiring it;

then we, who are still children, may justly feel it our highest duty to recognize the advisableness of improving natural knowledge, and so to aid ourselves and our successors in our course towards the noble goal that lies before mankind.[8]

Finally, we come to the views of Alfred Russell Wallace, the codiscoverer of the theory of evolution by natural selection, a man who might be known today as the first promulgator of that theory if he had sent his 1858 essay "On the Tendency of Varieties to Depart Indefinitely from the Original Type" directly to the *Annals and Magazine of Natural History* instead of sending it to Darwin. Although Wallace eventually became a believer in socialism and spiritualism and denied that man's distinctively human attributes could have been produced by natural selection, he was a good Spencerian in the late 1850s and early 1860s. At that time he accepted with few, if any, reservations the general views of nature, human nature, society, history, and science we have delineated as the basic tenets of "Darwinism." On September 29, 1862, shortly after his return to England from the Malay Archipelago, he wrote to Darwin: "I am now reading Herbert Spencer's 'First Principles,' which seems to me a truly great work, which goes to the root of everything." Soon afterward Wallace and his friend Henry Walter Bates called on Spencer to express their admiration for his "wonderful exposition of the fundamental laws and conditions, actions and interactions of the material universe" and to inquire whether he could throw any light on "the great unsolved problem of the origin of life." To their great disappointment Spencer could only say that life was undoubtedly "a development out of matter—a phase of that continuous process of evolution by which the whole universe had been brought to its present condition"—but that the problem of its origin was "too fundamental a problem to even think of solving at present."[9]

Wallace continued to draw inspiration from Spencer's writings, however, especially from the views on social evolution set forth in his *Social Statics*. In his essay "The Origin of Human Races and the Antiquity of Man Deduced from the Theory of 'Natural Selection,' " published in *The Anthro-*

pological Review in 1864, Wallace drew on his own and Darwin's theory of organic evolution by natural selection and on Spencer's theory of social evolution through competition and survival of the fittest to show (1) that the physical differences among the races of man must have developed millions of years ago, before the development of man's intellect and social sympathies had raised him above the power of natural selection by enabling him to adapt to changing circumstances culturally rather than physically, and (2) that, from that time onward, human evolution had necessarily consisted primarily of intellectual and moral advancement by means of a competitive struggle among individuals, tribes, and races in which the "better and higher specimens of our race" had increased and spread over the earth at the expense of the "lower and more brutal," driving them to extinction.

> It is the same great law of the "preservation of favoured races in the struggle for life" [Wallace wrote] which leads to the inevitable extinction of all those low and mentally undeveloped populations with which Europeans come in contact. The red Indian in North America, and in Brazil; the Tasmanian, Australian, and New Zealander in the southern hemisphere, die out, not from any one special cause, but from the inevitable effects of an unequal mental and physical struggle . . . just as the weeds of Europe overrun North America and Australia, extinguishing native productions by the inherent vigour of their organization, and by their greater capacity for existence and multiplication.

The final outcome of this process, Wallace prophesied, would be the blissful state envisaged by Herbert Spencer in *Social Statics*—a world inhabited by one homogeneous race of superior individuals, "no individual of which will be inferior to the noblest specimens of existing humanity."

> Each one will then work out his own happiness in relation to that of his fellows; perfect freedom of action will be maintained, since the well balanced moral faculties will never permit any one to transgress on the equal freedom of others; . . . compulsory government will have died away as unnecessary (for every man will know how to govern himself). . . ; the passions and animal

propensities will be restrained within those limits which most conduce to happiness; and mankind will have at length discovered that it was only required of them to develop the capacities of their higher nature, in order to convert this earth . . . into as bright a paradise as ever haunted the dreams of seer or poet.[10]

Wallace was later to point to this last sentence of his 1864 essay as a harbinger of his later non-Darwinian views concerning the agency of "higher intelligences" and a "higher law" in bringing about and directing human evolution. But there is little evidence from the period in which the essay was written to support such an interpretation. In the discussion that followed the reading of this essay before the Anthropological Society of London, Wallace's answer to Mr. Reddie's objection that he had not explained the origins of the human intellect was one that Darwin himself would have approved: "If Mr. Reddie denies that any animal has intellect, it is a difficult question to answer; but if animals have intellect in different proportions . . . I do not see the immense difficulty if you grant the universal process of selection from lower to higher animals." Indeed, Darwin was favorably impressed with the 1864 essay, which anticipated many of the ideas and arguments he was to develop later in *The Descent of Man*. "The latter part of the paper I can designate only as grand and most eloquently done," Darwin wrote to Wallace.

In 1869, by which time Wallace's views on human evolution had changed and had been made public in their new form, Wallace replied to Darwin's remonstrances against these new views as follows: "I can quite comprehend your feelings with regard to my 'unscientific' opinions as to Man, because a few years back I should myself have looked at them as equally wild and uncalled for. . . . My opinions on the subject have been modified solely by the consideration of a series of remarkable phenomena, physical and mental, which I have now had every opportunity of fully testing, and which demonstrate the existence of forces and influences not yet recognized by science."[11] Wallace was referring, of course, to spiritualistic phenomena, but it was not until the summer of 1865 that he witnessed any of these phenomena, according to

James Marchant. This would seem to indicate that his views on man were not modified before 1865. Even as late as October 1867, when he reviewed the Duke of Argyll's book *The Reign of Law* in the *Quarterly Journal of Science*, Wallace expounded an evolutionary deism indistinguishable from that which informs Darwin's *Origin of Species* and Spencer's *Social Statics*. Rejecting the Duke of Argyll's arguments for special creation, Wallace explains the theory of natural selection and concludes:

> It is very probable, that these primary facts or laws are but results of the very nature of life, and of the essential properties of organized and unorganized matter. Mr. Herbert Spencer, in his "First Principles" and his "Biology" has, I think, made us able to understand how this may be; but at present we may accept these simple laws without going further back, and the question then is—whether the variety, the harmony, the contrivance, and the beauty we perceive in organic beings, can have been produced by the action of these laws alone, or whether we are required to believe in the incessant interference and direct action of the mind and will of the Creator. It is simply a question of how the Creator has worked. . . . I believe . . . that the universe is so constituted as to be self-regulating; that as long as it contains Life, the forms under which that life is manifested have an inherent power of adjustment to each other and to surrounding nature; and that this adjustment necessarily leads to the greatest amount of variety and beauty and enjoyment, because it does depend on general laws, and not on a continual supervision and re-arrangement of details. As a matter of feeling and religion, I hold this to be a far higher conception of the Creator of the Universe than that which may be called the "continual interference" hypothesis. . . .[12]

Not until 1869 was Wallace ready to disavow natural selection as a sufficient cause of human evolution. When he republished his 1864 essay in 1870, he took pains to insert the phrase "from some unknown cause" in the following sentence: "But while these changes [differentiating the races physically] had been going on, his [man's] mental development had, *from some unknown cause*, greatly advanced, and had now reached that condition in which it began powerfully to influence his whole existence, and would therefore become subject to the irresistible action of 'natural selection' " (*italics mine*). And whereas in 1867 he had been content with a material universe "governed by unvarying law," in 1870 he was convinced "that the great laws which govern the material universe were insufficient for his [man's] production, unless we consider (as we may fairly do) that the controlling action of such higher intelligences is a necessary part of those laws. . . ." No wonder Darwin was inclined to "groan over Man" ("you write like a metamorphosed [in retrograde direction] naturalist, and you the author of the best paper that ever appeared in the *Anthropological Review*"), adding in a subsequent letter: "I must add that I have just re-read your article in the *Anthropological Review*, and I defy you to upset your own doctrine." Wallace had abandoned the Spencerian-Darwinian world view and was never to return to it.

From the foregoing discussion it should be apparent that Spencer, Darwin, Huxley, and Wallace reached similar views concerning nature, man, God, history, society, and science about 1860, converging on a world view that I propose to designate as Darwinism, although Spencer could rightfully demand that it be called Spencerianism. He had expounded its basic tenets, except the idea of organic evolution by natural selection, before 1859 and had championed the idea of competitive struggle and survival of the fittest as the motive force of social evolution by analogy to the "stern discipline of Nature" from 1850 onward. Each of these four men, in his own way, had fused several streams of Western thought into a unitary view of nature-history as a continuum undergoing progressive change in accordance with fixed laws discoverable by science. From the seventeenth-century revolution in physics and cosmology they derived their conception of nature as a wisely ordained, law-bound system of matter in motion. From Descartes, Kant, Laplace, and others they inherited the idea of deriving the present structures of the physical universe from a previous, more homogeneous state of the system of matter in motion through the operation of natural laws. From Hutton and Lyell they learned to view the surface of the earth as a material system producing perpetual changes in geological structures and constantly modifying the conditions of existence for living organisms. From Erasmus Darwin and Lamarck they got the idea that the wisely ordained system of nature was capable not merely of producing changes in the physical universe and in the conditions of life but also of generating simple organisms capable of undergoing progressive complication in structure and faculties in response to the demands of the changing environment, evolving man from a monad or living filament. From social theorists like Comte they acquired the vision of a social science of historical development that would discover the necessary laws and stages of human progress. From the British school of political economy and from British culture generally they derived their faith in the beneficent effects of competitive struggle. From Malthus, in particular, came their realization of the struggle for existence generated by the constant tendency of human populations to multiply beyond the means of subsistence. From the tradition of British empiricism and the positivistic currents of the nineteenth century they imbibed a sturdy faith in the methods of natural science as man's sole and sufficient means of acquiring knowledge of reality.

These were the ingredients, modified by Christian providentialism and natural theology and by the ubiquitous faith of the nineteenth century in progress, science, and technology, which combined in the thinking of Spencer, Darwin, Huxley, and Wallace to produce what Huxley called "the picture that science draws of the world": "Harmonious order governing eternally continuous progress—the web and woof of matter and force interweaving by slow degrees, without a broken thread, that veil which lies between us and the Infinite—that universe which alone we know or can know. . . ." At the time of the publication of Darwin's *Origin of Species* and Herbert Spencer's *First Principles* (1861), all four of these apostles of evolutionism were substantially agreed that this was indeed the picture that science drew of the world. Nor does it seem that any of them would have demurred from the idea that competitive struggle and survival of the fittest had been a primary, if not the chief, engine of progress in organic and social evolution.

In subsequent years Huxley was to reject completely Spencer's view of social progress as an outcome of competitive struggle, and Spencer himself was to conclude that the integration of simple groups into compound and doubly compound ones by military conquest had been carried "as far as seems either practicable or desirable." Meanwhile Wallace parted company with Spencer and Darwin on the subject of human evolution, defecting into spiritualism and socialism. Darwin himself leaned more heavily on use-inheritance in *The Descent of Man* than he had in his *Origin of Species*, but he seems to have remained more steadfast in his faith in the efficacy of natural selection in social evolution than any of the other three. In 1881, less than a year before his death, he expressed to William Graham his conviction that the Caucasian race had "beaten the Turkish hollow in the struggle for existence" and predicted that the "lower races" would soon be eliminated by the "higher civilized races" throughout the world. [13]

But these variations on and subsequent defections from the general view of nature, science, man, and history do not, it seems to me, invalidate the delineation of Spencerianism-Darwinism I have drawn for the early 1860s as a tool for the intellectual historian. In the controversies that ensued on the publication of the *Origin of Species* and *The Descent of Man*, the issues were many and varied, and "Darwinism" was defined variously by different writers according to the issues that were uppermost in their minds. To most people the crucial issue was whether organic evolution up to and including man by means of ordinary processes of nature had actually taken place. From this point of view Darwinism was simply evolutionism, and Darwin's theory was just another version of Lamarck's *Zoological Philosophy* and Robert Chambers's *Vestiges of the Natural History of Creation*. By those who accepted the idea of organic evolution but rejected Darwin's emphasis on natural selection as the main mechanism of evolution Darwinism was regarded as synonymous with the theory of natural selection, so as to distinguish it from Lamarckianism or neo-Lamarckianism. To men like Huxley, however, Darwinism was much more than a scientific theory. It was a view of the universe: "the picture which science draws of the world." So it was also to theologians like Charles Hodge and philosophers like the Duke of Argyll and Lord Balfour. These men were repelled as much by the deism verging toward agnosticism, the positivism, and the "scientific" materialism of the picture of the universe painted by Spencer and Huxley and shared less explicitly by Darwin as they were by the idea of organic evolution. Finally, to apologists for laissez-faire capitalism like William Graham Sumner, to advocates of late nineteenth-century imperialism like Karl Pearson, and even more so to the reformers who opposed these writers Darwinism was preeminently "social Darwinism," a doctrine Spencer had expounded nine years before Darwin published the *Origin of Species.*

These various uses of the word *Darwinism* are harmless enough when viewed against the full pattern of Spencerianism-Darwinism delineated above. Darwinism as a body of scientific theory is alive and flourishing in considerably modified form in our own day. Darwinism as a world view compounded of Cartesian mechanism, evolutionary deism fading into agnosticism, British empiricism verging toward positivism, and belief in progressive development through natural selection and the inherited effects of mental and moral training is also still with us, but in less robust condition. Darwinism as an ideology of social progress through competitive struggle of individuals, nations, tribes, and races is rejected in most quarters but not totally extinct. Like everything else, Darwinism evolves. Only a clear delineation of the elements that entered into its original constitution will enable us to trace its evolutionary history with any degree of certainty.*

---

*Of the various usages of the word *Darwinism*, the most common is that which identifies Darwinism with the theory of organic evolution by natural selection. I have given above (p. 128) my reasons for considering this an inadequate and in some respects misleading definition of Darwinism, but I should perhaps acquaint the reader with the arguments in its favor as explained to me in correspondence by Professor Ernst Mayr, a leading evolutionary biologist and a well-known writer on the history of evolutionary biology. Professor Mayr has kindly consented to let me quote from our correspondence. In his observations on an early draft of my paper he writes:

> Obviously, all of us absorb, and accept without thinking, a great many contemporary beliefs. The 1979 definitions of progress, equality, freedom, etc. are by no means the same as those held fifty or two hundred years ago, nor will they remain the same fifty years from now. There were quite a few contemporary ideas which Darwin accepted without asking questions but, in my opinion, they were not crucial for his basic paradigm, nor do we need to insist on retaining them if the term Darwinism is used at the end of the twentieth century. Most of these concepts were not at all typically Darwinian anyhow, and, as you rightly say, could be and probably should be called Spencerianism. You may make a few sociologists happy by inflicting that package of Spencerian concepts upon Darwin, but those who probably use the word Darwinism the most will simply ignore it. . . .
>
> The basic issue really is, whether it is legitimate to keep a package intact as it may have possibly existed in the 1870s (if your construction is correct). A term like Darwinism is bound to change in the course of time, just like terms such as equality, progress, or mutation, and to try to turn the clock back is not likely to be successful. No matter what you write, I am quite sure that everybody will continue to define Darwinism as the theory of evolution in which all directional change is caused by natural selection.

To this criticism I replied:

> It seems to me that there are several distinct questions that ought not to be confused: (1) Did Spencer, Darwin, Huxley, and Wallace share the constellation of beliefs I have attributed to them in the early 1860's? (2) if they did, what name should be used to designate this constellation of ideas? (3) if it is granted that Darwin shared these ideas, does it make sense to carry over the package of ideas (under whatever name) into the twentieth century, or should one select certain of Darwin's ideas that seem viable today and call them "Darwinism"?
>
> On the first question the only issue between us seems to be the extent to which Darwin shared the constellation of ideas I have attributed to Spencer, Huxley, and Wallace. (You do not seem to question that those three men shared these ideas.) Of the five ideas listed by me (p. 135) as constituting the constellation, you appear to be dubious chiefly about Darwin's acceptance of (1) "a unitary conception of nature-history as a law-bound system of matter in motion undergoing continual progress or

evolution from homogeneity toward heterogeneity," and (2) "evolutionary deism eventuating in agnosticism under the influence of positivistic conceptions of the sources of human knowledge." As to (2), I have already told you my reasons for believing that Darwin was an evolutionary deist up through the publication of the *Origin of Species*, and I find my position on this subject corroborated in Neal C. Gillespie's recent book *Charles Darwin and the Problem of Creation*. As you know, Gillespie is pretty much of my opinion about Darwin's religious beliefs and presents strong arguments for his views. You ask whether Darwin became an agnostic in the sense of admitting that he did not know whether there was a God or in the sense of affirming that man could *never* know whether there was a God. I think that the evidence is pretty conclusive that he eventually reached the latter position, as when he says that "a dog might as well speculate on the mind of Newton" as for a human being to speculate about the ultimate nature of reality. He had, he said, an "inward conviction" that the universe was not the result of mere chance. "But then," he added, "with me the horrid doubt always arises whether the convictions of man's mind, which has been developed from the mind of the lower animals, are of any value or at all trustworthy." Here it appears that his agnosticism flowed not only from positivistic conceptions of the sources of human knowledge but from his evolutionary naturalism with respect to the nature of man as well. It is interesting that Spencer, Huxley, Darwin, and Wallace were all brought up in a Christian environment, all became evolutionary deists (Huxley in a rather attenuated form), and all except Wallace wound up as agnostics, Wallace being saved from agnosticism by supposedly "scientific" evidence of a world of spirits. The main source of agnosticism in the nineteenth century was the positivistic current of thought that regarded science as man's only reliable means of gaining knowledge of reality, but in Darwin's case this positivistic outlook was reinforced by his own reflections on "the clumsy, wasteful, blundering, low, and horribly cruel" character of the process of natural selection and on the implications of a purely naturalistic evolutionary concept of man.

As to (1)—"a unitary conception of nature-history as a law-bound system of matter in motion undergoing continual progress or evolution from homogeneity toward heterogeneity"—I grant you that the words "from homogeneity toward heterogeneity" should be stricken from this; Spencer was the only one who pushed that idea. I also grant that Darwin was never as explicit as Huxley in embracing the Cartesian idea of nature as a law-bound system of matter in motion and linking it to the idea of organic evolution. Nevertheless Darwin says more than once that "everything is governed by fixed laws." In his letter to Asa Gray in 1860 he calls these "designed laws," an interesting evidence of his evolutionary deism as of that time. I pointed out in my book *The Death of Adam* (p. 305) that Darwin's theory of natural selection contained the germs of a probabilistic conception of order quite at odds with the mechanical determinism of nineteenth-century physics and chemistry, and that Charles Peirce and William James seized on this aspect of the theory as a means of deliverance from "the block universe eternal and without a history," as James called it. But I know of no evidence that Darwin himself or Huxley or Wallace appreciated this implication of the theory of natural selection. There was no room in their world for real chance. Huxley went so far as to observe that "None but parsons believe in chance. . . ."

I come now to the second main question: what name should be used to designate the constellation of ideas on which these men converged? This is a difficult problem because, although Spencer first synthesized these ideas in a coherent evolutionary view of reality, Darwin and Wallace supplied the empirically based theory of organic evolution that was indispensable in giving this view of reality a wide currency among educated people. And, because the prestige of science was reaching its high-water mark at that period, it was inevitable that Darwin's name, not Spencer's, should be attached to that view. To make matters worse, the word "Darwinism" came to be applied to other things as well: (1) the scientific theory (especially the idea of natural selection) espoused by Darwin and Wallace, (2) the general idea of organic evolution, (3) the notion of competitive struggle as the engine of progress in society as well as in nature. More recently Julian Huxley has tried to reserve the word "Darwinism" for the conception of scientific method he attributes to Darwin.

I am not sure what the solution to this problem in nomenclature is. Could we agree on "Spencero-Darwinism," or must we resort to Darwinism No. 1, Darwinism No. 2, etc.? You suggest cutting the Gordian knot by defining Darwinism as "the theory of evolution in which all directional change is caused by natural selection," and you assert that this definition is the one assumed by most twentieth-century biologists. But there are several difficulties in this. First, Darwin himself did not believe that all directional change is caused by natural selection. Second, Darwin's contemporaries, including Huxley, usually had in mind something much broader than the theory of natural selection when they spoke of Darwinism. Third, historians of ideas have usually distinguished between scientific theories and the isms connected with them. Fourth, for many twentieth-century biologists—Julian Huxley, George Gaylord Simpson, Edward O. Wilson, and others—Darwinism is a world view, not exactly the same world view as the one I have delineated but related to it through a process of descent-with-modification. From the point of view of the student of the history of ideas, the only sensible approach is to try to define the original senses of the term "Darwinism," explain how they were related to each other, and trace the subsequent history of the term.

Professor Mayr deserves the last word:

Let me admit to you at once that what evolutionary biologists now call Darwinism is not identical with Darwin's beliefs. After all, Darwin, up to his old age, believed in a certain amount of soft inheritance (use and dis-use, etc.), . . . was confused as to speciation, [and] often attributed to natural selection what is simply explained by common descent. . . . A historian obviously must bring out all these uncertainties, contradictions, and ambiguities. A scientist, working in the current framework of ideas, must redefine his terms continuously to keep up with the latest knowl-edge. . . . I have not been objecting to bringing out all of Darwin's hesitations, confusions and contradictions. However, when it comes to using terms that are common coin in modern science, we cannot load them down with the uncertainties of past history.

NOTES

1. Charles Darwin to Charles Lyell, Ilkley, Yorkshire, 25 Octo-ber 1859, quoted in *The Life and Letters of Charles Darwin*, ed. Francis Darwin, 3 vols. (London: John Murray, 1888), 2: 177.

2. Charles Darwin to Charles Lyell, Ilkley, Yorkshire, 11 Octo-ber 1859, quoted in ibid., 2: 211.

3. Charles Darwin to Asa Gray, 22 May 1860, quoted in ibid., 2: 311–312.

4. Charles Darwin, *The Descent of Man and Selection in Relation to Sex* (New York: D. Appleton and Co., 1896), p. 115.

5. Thomas H. Huxley, "Evolution in Biology," in *Darwiniana: Essays* (New York: D. Appleton, 1908), p. 206. First published in 1878.

6. Thomas H. Huxley, "The Origin of Species," in *Darwiniana: Essays*, p. 58. First published in 1860.

7. Thomas H. Huxley, "A Liberal Education," quoted in A. Castell, ed., *Selections from the Essays of T. H. Huxley* (New York: Appleton-Century-Crofts, 1948), p. 17.

8. Thomas H. Huxley, "On the Advisableness of Improving Natural Knowledge," quoted in Castell, *Essays of T. H. Huxley*, p. 15.

9. *Alfred Russel Wallace: Letters and Reminiscences*, James Mar-chant, ed., 2 vols. (New York and London: Harper and Bros., 1916), 2: 122; A. R. Wallace, *My Life: A Record of Events and Opinions*, 2 vols. (London: Chapman and Hall, 1905), 2: 23 ff.

10. Alfred Russell Wallace, "The Origin of Human Races and the Antiquity of Man Deduced from the Theory of 'Natural Selection'," *The Anthropological Review* 2 (1864): clxix–clxx. Also clxiii–clxv. This

essay was reprinted with significant additions and alterations in A. R. Wallace, *Contributions to the Theory of Natural Selection* (London and New York: Macmillan, 1870), pp. 302–331.

11. Wallace, *Letters and Reminiscences*, 2: 199–200. For Darwin's remonstrance, p. 206.

12. A. R. Wallace, "Creation by Law," in Wallace, *Theory of Natural Selection*, pp. 267–268. For the changes in the 1870 version of his 1864 essay, compare the former, pp. 320–321, with the latter, p. clxvi. See also Wallace's "The Limits of Natural Selection as Applied to Man," in *Theory of Natural Selection*, pp. 332–371.

13. Charles Darwin to William Graham, Down, 3 July 1881, quoted in *Life and Letters*, 1: 316.

SUGGESTED FURTHER READING

Most of the books and articles on Spencer, Darwin, Huxley, and Wallace deal with these writers individually rather than collectively, as in the present essay. However, William Irvine's *Apes, Angels, and Victorians* (New York: McGraw Hill, 1955) is a perceptive study of the relations between Darwin and Huxley. See also Robert Young's two essays: "Malthus and the Evolutionists: The Common Context of Biological and Social Theory," *Past and Present* no. 43 (1969): 109–145 and "The Historiographic and Ideological Contexts of the Nineteenth Century Debate on Man's Place in Nature," in M. Teich and R. Young, eds., *Changing Perspectives in the History of Science: Essays in Honour of Joseph Needham* (London: Heinemann, 1973), pp. 344–438. M. S. Helfand, "T. H. Huxley's Evolution and Ethics: The Politics of Evolution and the Evolution of Politics," *Victorian Studies* 20 (1977): 159–177, gives an excellent view of the political and social setting of the differences between Huxley, Spencer, and Wallace on the question of social ethics. There are good essays on Spencer and Huxley in A. O. J. Cockshut, *The Unbelievers: English Agnostic Thought, 1840–1890* (London: Collins, 1964). The changes in Huxley's views concerning nature, society, and ethics can be traced in Alburey Castell, ed., *Selections from the Essays of T. H. Huxley* (New York: Appleton-Century-Crofts, 1948) and in Oma Stanley, "T. H. Huxley's Treatment of 'Nature,' " *Journal of the History of Ideas* 18 (1957): 120–127. Gertrude Himmelfarb, *Victorian Minds* (London: Weidenfeld and Nicolson, 1968) has an excellent chapter on "Varieties of Darwinism." Two brief accounts of T. H.

Huxley's life and work are; Albert Ashforth, *Thomas Henry Huxley* (New York: Twayne Publishers, Inc., 1969) and Cyril Bibby, *T. H. Huxley: Scientist, Humanist, and Educator* (London: Watts and Co., 1959). The thesis of the present chapter is foreshadowed in John C. Greene, "The Concept of Order in Darwinism," in Paul G. Kuntz, ed., *The Concept of Order* (Seattle and London: University of Washington Press, 1968), pp. 89–103.

7

FROM HUXLEY TO HUXLEY: TRANSFORMATIONS IN THE DARWINIAN CREDO

What became of the Spencerian-Darwinian world view as the years passed and the nineteenth century gave way to the twentieth? As the previous essays have hinted, the outlook on nature, man, history, and society on which Spencer, Darwin, Wallace, and Huxley converged in 1860 began to show signs of stress almost as soon as it had taken form. Alarmed at the resurgence of militarism in Germany and the growing rivalry of nation states for colonial empire and military supremacy, Spencer called for a halt to the progressive integration of simple societies into compound and doubly compound ones by force of arms, expressing a pious hope that social progress would henceforth result from "the quiet pressure of a spreading industrial civilization on a barbarism which slowly dwindles."[1] Wallace, though still a staunch supporter of natural selection in nonhuman evolution, shocked the Darwinians by embracing spiritualism and socialism. Darwin clung tenaciously to his belief in natural selection as an engine of progress in both nature and history, but without ever resolving the conflict between the "higher morality" of Christianity and the brute exigencies of the severe struggle to which mankind must remain subject if it was to advance still further.

But it was Huxley in whom the conflicting demands of Victorian ethics and the harsh imperatives of natural selection, between the ironclad determinism of the law-bound system of matter in motion and the deeply felt sense of human freedom and moral responsibility, produced the severest strain. In the 1860s he had been sustained by a cheerful faith that nature's laws, however rigid, were the beneficent ordinances of a Master Intelligence who was "fair, just, and patient" and who was prepared to reward those who discovered and obeyed them. He could speak of "harmonious order governing eternally continuous progress" and exult in "Nature's great progression . . . from blind force to conscious intellect and will." He could argue that Darwin's theory left room for a "wider teleology" that found the element of design in the original structuring of the molecules constituting the primitive nebulosity of the universe. But he felt compelled to acknowledge that even if the primordial molecular arrangement had been wisely ordered to beneficent ends, it would still be impossible to say whether any particular result of the operations of the world machine was intended to be as it was or whether, instead, it was simply an incident of the functioning of the machine, like the ticking of a clock. To this question, Huxley declared, "there seems to be no reply . . . any more than to the further, not irrational question, why trouble one's self about matters which are out of reach, when the working of the mechanism itself, which is of infinite practical importance, affords scope for all our energies?"[2]

But if Huxley could thus put off the question of purpose in nature as being of little urgency to the scientist and the practical man, he could not evade the question of the basis of social ethics in a universe reduced to a "web and woof of matter and force interweaving by slow degrees, without a broken thread, that veil which lies between us and the Infinite—that universe which alone we know or can know," as he had described it in 1860. In 1868 he had conceived it to be the function of a liberal education to teach men the rules of Nature's game, to fashion their affections and wills "into an earnest and loving desire to move in harmony with those laws," to make them mouthpieces, ministers, and interpreters of Nature, their "ever-beneficent mother." By the time of his Romanes lecture in 1893, however, Huxley had parted company with those who tried to ground ethics in the cosmic process.

Laws and moral precepts are directed to the end of curbing the cosmic process and reminding the individual of his duty to the community, to the protection and influence of which he owes, if not existence itself, at least the life of something better than a brutal savage. . . . Let us understand, once for all [Huxley declared], that the ethical progress of society depends, not on imitating the cosmic process, still less in running away from it, but in combating it.[3]

But if ethical precepts were to be grounded neither in revelation nor in the cosmic process, where were they to find a solid basis? So far as Huxley answered this question, he seemed to fall back on the idea of moral intuition, invoking the maxims of the Hebrew prophets, especially Micah, as the sum and substance of human duty, though divorcing these maxims from their original religious inspiration.

The moral sense [he wrote to a friend] is a very complex affair—dependent in part upon associations of pleasure and pain, approbation and disapprobation formed by education in early youth, but in part also on an innate sense of moral beauty and ugliness (how originated need not be discussed), which is possessed by some people in great strength, while some are totally devoid of it. . . .
For the people with a keen innate sense of moral beauty there is no need of any other motive.[4]

This relapse into moral intuitionism rang strangely coming from the man who had earlier proclaimed that there was "but one kind of knowledge and but one method of acquiring it," and that the intellectual ethic derived from science forbade men to accept any proposition that could not be verified by observation and experiment.

Having arrived at a nonscientific basis for ethics, Huxley might well have faced a further question: How had a universe devoid of purpose or reason managed to produce a purposive, reasoning animal capable of setting himself at odds with the cosmic process that had produced him? The argument ended in paradox. On the one hand, man was a product of "the mutual interaction, according to definite laws, of the forces possessed by the molecules of which the primitive nebulosity of the universe was composed." Yet he was capable not only of comprehending the cosmic process but also of declaring war on it and seeking to negate its tendencies. Man was thus both the product and the antithesis of nature.

In these later essays of Huxley we pass beyond the Spencerian-Darwinian identification of man and nature and the concomitant idea that human evolution, like biological evolution, has a built-in mechanism ensuring eventual progress through improvement in the intellectual and instinctual endowment of the surviving races; we pass beyond that idea to a dawning appreciation of the uniqueness of man, of his ambivalent status as part of, yet at the same time *not* a part of nature, as a moral being not bound by natural necessity. Huxley was explicit on this point. "That progressive modification of civilization which passes by the name of the 'evolution of society,' " he wrote, "is, in fact, a process of an essentially different character both from that which brings about the evolution of species in the state of nature, and from that which gives rise to the evolution of [domestic] varieties in the state of art."[5] Aware that man might conceivably plan his own genetic future, directing its progress through eugenic controls, Huxley drew back from that terrifying prospect. No man, he declared, has sufficient intelligence to select the human beings fittest to survive and propagate. And even if some group acquired the requisite intelligence, what would be the consequences of entrusting them with so awful a power? "I do not see how such selection could be practiced without a serious weakening, it may be the destruction, of the bonds which hold society together," Huxley warned.[6]

One wonders what this sadder and wiser Huxley would have said if he could have seen Darwin's letter of 1881 touting natural selection as "having done and doing more for the progress of civilization" than most men were willing to admit and predicting that natural selection would soon bring about the elimination of the "lower races" by the "higher civilized races" throughout the world. Huxley's own ultimate wisdom was of a more traditional sort:

> That which lies before the human race [he declared] is a constant struggle to maintain and improve, in opposition to the State of Nature, the State of Art and of organized polity; in which, and by

which, man may develop a worthy civilization, capable of maintaining and constantly improving itself; until the evolution of our globe shall have entered so far upon its downward course that the cosmic process resumes its sway; and, once more, the State of Nature prevails over the surface of our planet.[7]

A Greek might have written that!

In the half century and more separating the writings of Thomas Henry Huxley from those of his grandson Julian Huxley, striking changes in both science and world view took place. For a considerable time Darwin's theory of evolution by means of natural selection found little favor among biologists and paleontologists. Evolution carried the day, but mutationism, orthogenesis, and various forms of neo-Lamarckianism overshadowed natural selection as the putative mechanisms of organic change. Finally, in the 1930s and 1940s, the leading developments in cytology, genetics, taxonomy, biogeography, and paleontology were brought together in a new synthesis centered on the theory of natural selection. Darwinism had been reborn, Julian Huxley announced in his *Evolution: The Modern Synthesis* (1943). Darwin's faith in natural selection as the primary agent in evolution had been vindicated. Expounded in the writings of Huxley, Ernst Mayr, Theodosius Dobzhansky, Bernard Rensch, George Gaylord Simpson, J. B. S. Haldane, Ronald Fisher, Sewall Wright, and others, the "modern synthesis" triumphed and soon became the new orthodoxy.

But what of Darwinism as a world view? Has the new, modified Darwinian biology brought with it a modified "Darwinian" outlook on nature, man, society, and history? Indeed it has. The twentieth-century protagonists of the modern synthesis have produced a spate of writings bearing such titles as *Evolution in Action*, *The Meaning of Evolution*, *This View of Life*, *Nature and Man's Fate*, *The Ethical Animal*, *On Human Nature*, and the like, purporting to explain the significance of evolutionary biology for human duty and destiny. Although their authors would probably deny it, these books are the Bridgewater Treatises* of the twentieth century, in that they seek to find in science indications and proofs concerning ultimate questions of meaning and value. According to Julian Huxley, "the destiny of man on earth has been made clear by evolutionary biology. . . . man can now see himself as the sole agent of further evolutionary advance on this planet, and one of the few possible instruments of progress in the universe at large."[8] Likewise, George Gaylord Simpson advertises evolutionary biology as the only discipline that can provide objective answers to such "big and real" questions as: Who am I? What am I doing here? What is the world? What is my relationship to it? "By consciously seeking what was most meaningful," Simpson explains to his readers, "I moved from poetry to mineralogy to paleontology to evolution."[9] The answers to the problem of life's meaning provided by evolutionary biology, he adds, will take the place of the lower and higher superstitions that have served mankind till now.

In view of these far-reaching claims for the religious and moral significance of evolutionary biology, it seems imperative to ask what lessons these writers have drawn from their study of evolution and to compare them with the lessons garnered by Spencer, Darwin, Wallace, and Huxley. If we begin with such a work as Julian Huxley's *Evolution in Action* (1953), we have the impression at first of reentering the world of Herbert Spencer. Once again we are dazzled with the prospect of an evolutionary science embracing the whole of cosmic, organic, and cultural evolution in a single continuum of progressive development. Evolutionary science, Julian Huxley tells us, draws on physics, chemistry, cosmology, geology, biology, archaeology, anthropology, and psychology and enables man to see his own history in its proper relationship with the history of the universe as a whole. We

---

*In 1825 the Earl of Bridgewater made provision in his will for a series of works "On the Power, Wisdom, and Goodness of God, as manifested in the Creation."

are even provided with a "scientific" and "objective" definition of progress in the biological realm. To arrive at this definition, Huxley postulates a linear succession of dominant forms: fishes, reptiles and insects, mammals, man. He then examines the characteristics that distinguish dominant from nondominant fauna and sums them up under two heads: (1) greater efficiency in dealing with the environment and (2) greater independence of the environment, through internal temperature regulation and similar "improvements in the machinery of living." "Advance in these respects," says Huxley, "may provisionally be taken as the criterion of progress." By this criterion, man is obviously the most progressive animal, since he is preeminent in control and independence of the environment. "Man *is* the latest dominant type to be evolved, and this being so, we are justified in calling the trends which have led to this development *progressive.*"[10]

But why, we may ask, should increased control and independence of the environment be regarded as constituting progress? Presumably because they enhance the organism's chances of survival. So, too, with Huxley's criterion of biological efficiency: efficiency with respect to the accomplishment of what ends? Presumably the ends of survival and reproduction. Huxley distinguishes between adaptations that constitute "an improvement in efficiency of adaptation for a particular mode of life" and those that bring about "an improvement in efficiency of living in general." In either case, however, the only end or value biologically speaking is survival, either of a particular form of life or of life in general. From a strictly biological point of view it seems difficult to get away from survival as the basic value or to derive any concept of progress that does not boil down to survival or likelihood of survival.[11]

Faced with this dilemma, Huxley seeks a way out by envisaging evolution—cosmic, biological, cultural—as an "over-all process of realizing new possibilities of variety and organization." Gone now is Herbert Spencer's ironclad system of matter in motion: "the bogey of causal determinism," Huxley calls it. Instead, reality is a creative process, "unitary, continuous, irreversible; self-transforming; and generating variety and novelty during its transformations."[12] This is the language of modern process philosophy, but note that Huxley excludes from the process all those elements—aim, purpose, creative ground—which run counter to the positivistic grain of modern science and which alone could make such a process intelligible. The result is that Julian Huxley, like his grandfather, propounds the paradox that nature, though devoid of aim and purpose, yet moves toward ever higher levels of order and value.

Like Spencer, Huxley conceives psychosocial evolution (what Spencer called superorganic evolution) as a continuation of organic evolution, but he rejects completely Spencer's mechanisms of use-inheritance and natural selection. Use-inheritance, he declares, has been disproved by the science of genetics, and natural selection is irrelevant to social evolution. "The human situation is so different from the biological," Sir Julian writes, "that it may prove best to abandon the attempt to apply concepts like natural selection to modern human affairs."[13] Intraspecific competition, he asserts, is *never* productive of progressive change, hence all notions of progress through individual, racial, and national competition must be discarded.

Nevertheless, although Huxley refuses to conceive cultural evolution in terms of natural selection, he does suggest that other biological analogies will prove useful in understanding it. Religious beliefs, ethical ideals, and scientific theories are described as "tools of living." And just as there are extinct species and progressive and nonprogressive forms of life, so there are extinct cultures, progressive and nonprogressive cultures. A progressive culture is one that "contains the seeds of its own further transformation." Cultures that are not "in some way related to the general trends of the human process" may become "a drag on the advance of humanity as a whole," but they are to be preserved as "living fossils" instead of being waved a sad farewell on the road to extinction, as Spencer and Darwin seemed to suggest.

Apart from these vague analogies, the only common property of cosmic, biological, and social evolution for Huxley is the fact that they all involve "the realization of possibilities," a property even more general than Spencer's universal trend toward increasing heterogeneity. Doubtless everything that comes into existence existed as a possibility beforehand, but how this helps us to understand either cosmic, biological, or social evolution is not clear. At the biological level Huxley stresses natural selection as the process responsible for progress toward higher forms of existence. In psychosocial evolution, he tells us, the struggle for existence has been replaced by the struggle for fulfillment. Fulfillment means "the realization of inherent capacities by the individual and of new possibilities by the race; the satisfaction of needs, spiritual as well as material; the emergence of new qualities of experience to be enjoyed; the building of personalities"—all to be achieved in a struggle not merely with external obstacles but also with "the enemies within our own selves."[14]

Recognizing, however, that not all possibilities are good, not all fulfillments desirable, Huxley faces at last the question of the basis of ethics. On this issue he sides with Spencer rather than his grandfather. Like Spencer, he seeks to ground morality in the cosmic process. The essence of evolution, Huxley writes, is the realization of ever new possibilities. It follows that man's duty and destiny is "to be the agent of the world process of evolution, the sole agent capable of leading it to new heights, and enabling it to realize new possibilities. . . ." Whatever permits or promotes "open development" is good; whatever restricts or frustrates it is wrong. Social and cultural institutions, including the state, are instruments for enabling individuals to fulfill themselves. So, too, is evolutionary science. Eugenics can promote human progress by strengthening physical vigor, preventing hereditary defects and diseases, and raising the general level of intelligence and aptitude. In like manner, the scientific study of man's inner life can make available to the common man the transcendent states of inner peace and unity experienced by mystics and yogis. The more immediate problems of war, famine, disease, exploitation, and ethnocentrism present great difficulties, Huxley admits, but they, too, will eventually be brought under control by evolutionary science guided by "the morality of evolutionary direction." Man is in the process of becoming "business manager for the cosmic process of evolution," and he may be trusted to carry out his responsibilities in the long run.

> Man is very young. . . . man is the result of two thousand million years of biological evolution: he has every prospect of an equal or even greater span of psycho-social evolution before him. The human species has many grave problems before it: but it has a great deal of time in which to work them out—there may be some comfort in that thought.[15]

Thus, for Huxley as for Spencer, evolutionary science is the key to the riddle of human destiny. In Huxley's view, this science has shown conclusively that man's destiny is "to participate and lead in the creative process of evolution, where new possibilities can be realized for life." Nothing, he says, can be more important to mankind "in an age of doubt and transition like the present" than to see its destiny and duty in this light. "Only by getting some over-view of reality, in its dual aspect of self-transforming pattern and continuing process," Huxley concludes, "can man hope to get a clearer view of his place—his unique place—and steer a better course into the future."[16]

Here again, as in the case of his grandfather, one is struck by the paradoxes in Huxley's thinking. Apart from man, the cosmic process has no aim, yet it realizes ever higher possibilities until it produces man, who then acquires a moral obligation to lead the cosmic process farther in a direction it does not know it is going. But the ultimate paradox is that man's vaunted "independence and control of the environment," which Huxley invokes as proof that evolution is progressive, now threatens to become the instrument of man's destruction as he moves toward making the environment uninhabitable not only for himself but for other living creatures as well.

Actually, of course, mankind has never been independent of or in control of the environment, especially if one includes the human environment, as surely one must. Man shows little sign of becoming master of his destiny, of controlling the course of social evolution, to say nothing of biological and cosmic evolution. The multiplication of devices and techniques for controlling the natural environment and influencing human behavior seems only to aggravate man's lack of control over the general course of events and to intensify the moral problems connected with human freedom. Cultural evolution may indeed involve the realization of possibilities, but the possibilities for evil multiply as rapidly as the possibilities for good, and history affords little assurance that men and women, either individually or collectively, will choose the general welfare of mankind in preference to immediate personal or national advantage. If man is in truth "business manager for the cosmic process of evolution," the future of the cosmic enterprise is in precarious condition. Whom the gods would destroy they first make mad.

If Julian Huxley is the Herbert Spencer of twentieth-century Darwinism, George Gaylord Simpson may in some ways be considered its Thomas Henry Huxley. A paleontologist, agnostic, and inquirer into the history of evolutionary thought like the elder Huxley, Simpson has played a leading role in marshalling the resources of paleontology in support of the modern synthetic theory of evolution, in waging war against vitalistic and finalistic interpretations of the fossil record, and in championing evolutionary science as the only sure guide to a knowledge of human duty and destiny. In his paleontological polemics his main purpose has been to show that organic evolution is a "materialistic" process that displays no inherent tendency toward movement in any particular direction. As a moralist, he is concerned to demonstrate that evolutionary science, and it alone, yields an intellectual ethic adequate to human needs. As a historian of evolutionary thought, he seeks to display the modern synthetic theory as incorporating the insights of Lamarck, Darwin, the neo-Darwinists, the mutationists, and the neo-Lamarckians while eliminating their errors.

All these themes are brought together and interwoven in Simpson's Terry Lectures at Yale, entitled *The Meaning of Evolution* and published in 1949, six years after Huxley's

Evolution: The Modern Synthesis with its concluding chapter "Evolutionary Progress." Like the authors of the Bridgewater Treatises a century earlier, the Terry Lecturers were charged to discourse on the relations of science and religion. And just as the nineteenth-century authors undertook to discover the divine attributes in the creation, so Simpson, following in Julian Huxley's steps, set out to find moral and spiritual guidance for mankind in the workings of evolution. His task was not an easy one, for he was precluded both by his paleontological and by his religious convictions from representing evolution as the working out of either an immanent or a transcendent purpose. Science, he insists, deals only with the causal analysis of material phenomena, as in the modern synthetic theory of evolution.

> This is not to say that the whole mystery has been plumbed to its core or even that it ever will be. The ultimate mystery is beyond the reach of scientific investigation, and probably of the human mind. There is neither need nor excuse for postulation of non-material intervention in the origin of life, the rise of man, or any other part of the long history of the material cosmos. Yet the origin of the cosmos and the causal principles of its history remain unexplained and inaccessible to science. Here is hidden the First Cause sought by theology and philosophy. The First Cause is not known and I suspect that it never will be known to living man. We may, if we are so inclined, worship it in our own ways, but we certainly do not comprehend it.[17]

Like Spencer, Huxley, and the later Darwin, Simpson is an agnostic. It is important to him, therefore, both as a scientist and as an agnostic, to show that the fossil record lends no support to the idea that evolutionary processes have a directional tendency as earlier American paleontologists like Edward Drinker Cope and Henry Fairfield Osborn maintained. On a limited scale this issue turns on the interpretation of observed trends in the evolution of particular groups of animals, such as the horse family. Do these trends require one to postulate an immanent tendency toward change in a given direction, or can they be explained as the outcome of random variation and natural selection? In a more general sense, however, the issue concerns the problem of "progress" in the overall evolution of life. On this question Simpson displays a certain ambivalence. As a paleontologist he cannot accept Julian Huxley's linear sequence of dominant forms leading to man or his criterion of progress based on independence and control of the environment.

> We do not . . . find successive dominance between, say Osteichthyes [bony fishes], Aves [birds], and Mammalia. All three [writes Simpson] are dominant at the same time, during the Cenozoic and down to now. Taking the animal kingdom as a whole, it is clearly necessary to add insects, molluscs, and also the "lowly" Protozoa as groups now dominant. If one group had to be picked as most dominant now, it would have to be the insects, but the fact is that all these groups are fully dominant, each in a different sphere.[18]

As for "independence and control of the environment," says Simpson, this turns out to mean ability to cope with a wide variety of environments rather than independence of the environment as a whole. And so it is with various other criteria of progress proposed by biologists and paleontologists: for instance, successive invasion and development of biological spheres, replacement within adaptive zones, improvement in adaptation, potentiality for further progress, complication of structure, increase in general energy, increase in awareness and reactivity to environmental stimuli, and the like. In Simpson's opinion, none of these criteria provides a basis for describing and ordering the evolutionary process as a whole.

> Evolution is not invariably accompanied by progress, nor does it really seem to be characterized by progress as an essential feature. Progress has occurred within it but is not of its essence. Aside from the broad tendency for the expansion of life, which is also inconstant, there is no sense in which it can be said that evolution *is* progress. Within the framework of the evolutionary history of life there have been not one but many different sorts of progress. Each sort appears not with one single line or even with one central but branching line throughout the course of evolution, but separately in many different lines. These phenomena seem fully consistent with, and indeed readily explained by, the materialistic theory of evolution. . . . They are certainly inconsistent with

the existence of a supernal perfecting principle, with the concept of a goal in evolution, or with control of evolution by autonomous factors, a vital principle common to all forms of life.[19]

The basic characteristic of evolution, says Simpson, is for life to expand into every available niche, creating new niches for occupation as it evolves. Blind "opportunism," not plan or purpose, is the hallmark of evolution.

Yet, having thus dimissed progress as a characteristic of the evolutionary process, Simpson seems reluctant to abandon the concept entirely. Conceding that none of the various criteria of progress characterizes evolution as a whole, he nevertheless attempts to establish man's credentials as the most progressive animal by showing that he rates very high by most of these criteria.

> Progress [he writes] does exist in the history of life, but is of many different sorts and each sort occurs separately in many different lines. One sort of progress in structure and function that stands out as particularly widespread and important is increasing awareness of the life situation of the individual organism and increasing variety and sureness of appropriate reactions to this. Among the many different lines that show progress in this respect, the line leading to man reaches much the highest level yet developed. By most other criteria of progress, also, man is at least among the higher animals and a balance of considerations fully warrant considering him definitely the highest of all.
>
> Man is the result of a purposeless and materialistic process that did not have him in mind. He was not planned.[20]

Thus, Simpson arrives at the paradoxical conclusion that the evolutionary process, though devoid of aim and purpose or any inherent progressive tendency, has nevertheless produced an animal, man, who has aims and purposes and who somehow or other deserves to be considered the "most progressive product of evolution." He even points out certain diagnostic features—intelligence, flexibility, individualization, and socialization—which, he says, make man different in kind as well as degree from other animals. But why do these features deserve to be called "progressive?" From a biological point of view they confer on man "increased and improved means of perception of the environment and, particularly, of integrating, coordinating, and reacting flexibly to these perceptions"—in other words, they increase his chances of survival as a species. Doubtless survival is better than extinction biologically speaking, but does it constitute an adequate criterion of progress? Simpson admits that progress must be defined "not merely as movement but as movement in a direction from (in some sense) worse to better, lower to higher, or imperfect to more nearly perfect."[21] How, then, is the biologist to define better and worse, higher and lower?

Like his predecessors, Simpson is caught in the perennial dilemma of the biologist who, as a human being, seeks to impart meaning to the evolutionary process by regarding it as a progress toward higher things but who, as a scientist trained in the cult of objectivity, finds it impossible to define progress scientifically without reducing it to mere survival or potentiality for survival. As a scientist, he can say of the idea of progress what Laplace said to Napoleon of the idea of God: "Sire, I have no need of that hypothesis." But as a human being seeking meaning and value in the universe and in science itself he cannot do without the idea of progress unless he has some alternative clue to the problem of meaning. Simpson's positivistic agnosticism leaves no room for any such alternative.

In this difficult situation Simpson finds a way out by resorting to the same expedients that served Julian Huxley well under similar conditions. First, he portrays life, or "life substance," metaphorically as exploiting its opportunities, solving problems, inventing novel and successful types of organization, "trying out every conceivable possibility," "pulling through" various "crises" in its history, and ultimately transcending itself by producing an animal, man, capable of undergoing a totally new type of evolution guided by "interthinking" rather than interbreeding. Like T. H. Huxley, he celebrates "Nature's great progression . . . from blind force to conscious intellect and will." Second, he endows evolutionary biology with moral significance by representing it as the only true basis of a rational ethics. He agrees, however, with T. H.

Huxley that ethics cannot be derived from prehuman evolution:

> It is futile to search for an absolute ethical criterion retroactively in what occurred before ethics themselves evolved [Simpson declares]. The best human ethical standard must be relative and particular to man and is to be sought rather in the new evolution, peculiar to man, than in the old, universal to all organisms. The old evolution was and is essentially amoral. The new evolution involves knowledge, including the knowledge of good and evil.[22]

The essential characteristic of the new evolution, says Simpson, is "knowledge, together . . . with its spread and inheritance."

> As a first proposition of evolutionary ethics derived from specifically human evolution, it is submitted that promotion of knowledge is essentially good. This is the basic material ethic. . . . Knowledge is of many sorts and is to be sought in no one way. . . . Science is, however, our most successful and systematic means of acquiring knowledge and, at present, almost alone in the power to acquire knowledge wholly new to man.[23]

There are echoes here of T. H. Huxley's early essay "On the Advisability of Improving Natural Knowledge," with its picture of the "intellectual ethic" generated by the progress of science. But Simpson, like Huxley, recognizes that scientific knowledge can be used for evil as well as good. This, in turn, implies some criterion of good and evil other than the increase of natural knowledge. Science, says Simpson, yields not only the ethic of knowledge but also "the still more fundamental ethic of responsibility," an ethic that makes scientists individually responsible for evaluating the knowledge they acquire and for "its ultimate utilization for good." Man's responsibility, he adds, is really not an ethic but a *fact*, "a fundamental and peculiar characteristic of the human species established by his evolution and evident in his relationship to the rest of the cosmos."

> Man is . . . the responsible animal. This is more basic than his knowledge, although dependent on it, for some other animals

surely know and think in a way not completely inhuman, but no other animal can truly be said to be responsible in anything like the same sense in which man is responsible.[24]

These explanations raise more difficulties than they solve. To whom is man responsible? To the blind forces that produced him? To life? To the "new evolution" of which he is the sole agent? To the human species, which he knows to be an accidental product of planless, purposeless processes? To the last of these, apparently:

> The first grand lesson learned from evolution was that of the unity of life. One of the great ethical achievements of early Christianity and some of the other religions was recognition, in principle, of the brotherhood of man. While it refuted certain other intuitive conclusions of various Christian and other theologians, confirmation of the truth of evolution established this doctrine as a scientific fact. . . . Not only are all men brothers; all living things are brothers in the very real, material sense that all have arisen from one source and been developed within the divergent intricacies of one process.[25]

Thus, despite his declared intention to ground ethics solely on human evolution, Simpson, like Julian Huxley, is driven to base it on the total evolutionary process, the "facts" of which are interpreted as implying the validity of the noblest ideals and aspirations of the human spirit. The dignity and sanctity of the individual vis-à-vis the claims of the totalitarian state, says Simpson, are rooted in "another human evolutionary characteristic, that of high individualization." If the evolutionary process produces a trend toward individualization, the individual is sacred. If it produces animals capable of choice, they have a responsibility to choose "rightly." If all men and animals are descended from common ancestors, the brotherhood of man is a valid moral concept, even though evolution itself operates by random variation, struggle for existence, and the remorseless elimination of unfit individuals, races, and species.

Strange logic! To the outside observer it seems obvious that Simpson and Huxley simply take for granted the moral values and ideals of Western culture and seek to derive them from some other source than the sources that originally inspired them—Greek culture and the Judeo-Christian tradition. They are forced to do so because they reject both philosophy and Christianity as incompatible with the positivistic conception of knowledge that informs all their thinking. Like the early T. H. Huxley, they incline toward the view that "there is but one kind of knowledge and one way of acquiring it." But, if this were true, science itself would have to provide answers to the age-old problem of human duty and destiny. It would have to furnish both the scientific and the ethical guidance needed to guarantee that mankind will progress instead of retrogressing.

Like Julian Huxley, Simpson is cautiously optimistic that science will be able to fulfill these responsibilities. He concedes that the social sciences, on which rests the main responsibility for guiding human progress, are "themselves the lumber room of ethics, crowded with old, conflicting, and certainly partly false ethical systems and the battleground of these."

> We need desperately to know [says Simpson] more about our-selves, about our societies, about all of life, about the earth, and about the universe. We need to balance our knowledge better, to reverse the disparity in discovery in the physical, biological, and social sciences so that the social sciences shall be first and the physical last. . . . We need, too, to recognize the supreme impor-tance of knowledge of organic and of social evolution. Such knowledge provides most of what we know of our place in the universe and it must guide us if we are to control the future evolution of mankind.[26]

Here again, as with Julian Huxley, the prospect is held out that mankind will become business manager for the evolu-tionary process. Here again eugenics (by "voluntary indi-vidual actions" rather than by compulsion) is recommended as a means of furthering progress by improving human intelligence. Like Francis Galton a century earlier, Simpson is convinced that "the most brilliant men simply do not have enough learning capacity to acquire all the details of more than increasingly narrow segments of the field of knowledge." "Only a very stupid person can believe that mankind is already intelligent enough for its own good."[27] Simpson concedes that scientists at present do not know how to produce to order "the sort of mutation that may be needed or desired." But if and when man discovers this secret, "then indeed evolution will pass fully into his control."

Simpson's faith in the beneficent effects of the exponential growth of scientific knowledge is breathtaking. Aware that man may blow himself off the face of the earth, he argues that this danger has arisen only because the physical sciences discovered the secret of atomic energy before the social sciences learned how to ensure the ethical application of this knowledge. It never occurs to him that scientific knowledge of the hidden springs of individual and social action could be as dangerous to human welfare as knowledge of the structure of the atom. What price would any dictator not pay for such knowledge! Like Julian Huxley, Simpson is buoyed by a serene faith in the ultimate beneficence of scientific knowledge and the ultimate goodness of man. Man, he writes, was "certainly not the goal of evolution, which evidently had no goal." Nevertheless, he represents "the most highly endowed organization of matter that has yet appeared on the earth—and we certainly have no good reason to believe there is any higher in the universe"; and he must prove himself worthy of his "high endowment."

The paradoxes in this view of things are staggering. Man is an accidental product of a planless, purposeless process, yet he is "highly endowed" and morally obligated to "rise still farther" in a world that supplies no criterion of "higher" or "lower" nor any impetus toward progress in any particular direction. Spawned by an amoral universe, man yet has the knowledge of good and evil. The result of causally determined, material processes of nature, he is nevertheless free to chart his future course by scientific control over those processes or to destroy himself by perverting his knowledge to selfish ends.

But if human evolution—the "new evolution"—is really as different from organic evolution as Simpson maintains, if man is different from other animals in kind as well as in degree, then what is the relevance of evolutionary biology to the question of human duty and destiny? And is the attempt of modern evolutionary biologists to provide answers to this question from their scientific findings not as futile and delusory as were the efforts of William Buckland, Adam Sedgwick, and Benjamin Silliman to demonstrate the existence and attributes of God from the record of the rocks? In both cases, the conclusions antedate the investigation and dictate its outcome. Simpson and Huxley did not learn to value the individual, to detest totalitarianism, and to believe in the brotherhood of man from studying biology and paleontology any more than Buckland and his contemporaries learned to believe in an omnipotent, omniscient, and benevolent Creator from their scientific researches. One group of scientists approached nature as agnostics or atheists, the other as Christians; each found what it expected to find. Each had a moral commitment, the first to vindicate the values they held dear and discredit beliefs they regarded as inimical to the further progress of science, the second to confound skeptics and corroborate religious doctrines that made human duty and destiny intelligible to them. In both cases science was only a tool, a weapon, in defense of positions that were essentially religious and philosophical. Faith in science can be no less a religion than faith in God.

In *This View of Life: The World of an Evolutionist*, published fifteen years after *The Meaning of Evolution*, Simpson appears as convinced as ever that evolutionary biology contains the answers to the "big and real" questions of human duty and destiny, answers that will replace those hitherto supplied by the "lower" and "higher" superstitions (Christianity being an example of the latter). But he seems uneasy about the rise of molecular biology and the tendency of its cultivators to reduce biology to physics and chemistry, to take the *bios* out of biology, and thereby to displace evolutionary biology as the key to scientific understanding of man's place in nature. Responding to this threat, Simpson argues that it was biologists who discovered the role of genes and bid the chemists study nucleic acids. The chemists then discovered DNA, but this knowledge, says Simpson, "has as yet cast almost no further light on what genes do *in terms of the organism*." Besides, DNA was itself constructed by natural selection in the course of organic evolution. Contrasting the claims of "egg-evolutionists" (molecular biologists) and "hen-evolutionists" (organismal biologists), Simpson writes:

> Perhaps I have a bias toward hen-evolution and organismal biology, but to me this is far the most important thing about the genetic message. Is it not more important to know what Shakespeare said and how he wrote his message than to analyze it into the letters of the alphabet or even the words of the dictionary?[28]

In keeping with this holistic view, Simpson goes on to question the claim of physics to constitute the fundamental science of nature and to insist on a certain amount of teleology in the interpretation of nature. Long before quantum theory taught physicists that their predictions were statistical, their laws not invariable, biologists knew about statistical laws and polymodal causality, Simpson declares. Long before physicists discovered that observations are influenced by the process of observation, biologists knew that the organism and the environment, the inner and outer worlds, were interdependent. Science itself, they realized, was fundamentally biological, a part of animal behavior. And, most important of all, biologists recognized the teleological aspect of living organisms and the consequent necessity of adding a "compositionist" form of explanation to the reductionist explanations of physicists and chemists. Darwin pointed the way by redefining teleology as the study of adaptation, thereby substituting scientific teleology for a philosophical or theological one.

> This second form of explanation . . . is in terms of the adaptive usefulness of structures and processes to the whole organism and to the species of which it is a part, and still further, in terms of ecological function in the communities in which the species occurs. It is still scientifically meaningful to say that . . . a lion has its thoroughgoing adaptations to predation *because* they maintain the life of the lion, the continuity of its species, and the economy of its communities.
>
> Such statements exclude the grosser, man-centered forms of teleology, but they still do not necessarily exclude a more impersonal philosophical teleology.[29]

The physicists, says Simpson, have sought to achieve the unification of the sciences by finding principles of increasing generality applicable to all material processes. In so doing, they have been forced to "falsify nature" and ignore the actual complexity of things. A better way of unifying the sciences would be to search for phenomena to which all principles apply. From this point of view, declares Simpson, biology is "the science that stands at the center of all science."[30]

In these arguments, Simpson has come a long way from his earlier "materialistic," antiteleological position. Carried to its logical conclusion, his reasoning would force him to admit that human beings, conceived not simply as biological organisms but as persons and communities of persons, are the most complex beings known to man and hence are the phenomena to which all principles apply, including principles extraneous to biology. In that case, the science of the human psyche would stand at the center of all science, and biology would take its place at a lower level of investigation. But Simpson's materialistic positivism prevents him from recognizing the difference between a human being as a biological organism and a human being as a person. He wants to have his cake and eat it—to banish reductionism as applied to biology but insist on it as applied to man. He is ready to yield first place in importance to the sciences of man but unwilling to concede that human nature has dimensions that transcend the scope of science as he understands it. What he concedes in the name of organismal biology he takes back at the behest of outdated and inadequate conceptions of science and of man.

Neither Julian Huxley nor George Gaylord Simpson had any use for Darwin's idea that natural selection was operative in human history.[31] But one of the champions of the modern synthetic theory of evolution, the British geneticist Cyril Darlington, wrote a 700-page book, *The Evolution of Man and Society*, designed to substantiate Darwin's faith in natural selection "having done and doing more for the progress of civilization" than most people realized. According to Darlington, natural selection acting on the hominoid brain "determined the character of modern human societies and prepared for the upheaval which brought the paleolithic world to an end." The improvement of the brain, in turn, came about because improved brains were advantageous to individuals of a species equipped with hands that could make tools. Building on the argument of Darwin's *Descent of Man*, Darlington explains that:

> Every improvement in the brain that guided the work of the hands in making the tools, in using the tools, and in foreseeing new uses and new makes, was bound to be advantageous—almost without limit—to the individuals improved. . . . Differences in these improvements are still today subject to selective survival. . . . Each invention propagates its own inventors and leads to their multiplication, and expansion. And these in turn lead to their hybridization with other stocks and the production of yet more genetic combinations with similarly enhanced capacities.[32]

It was in the central land masses of the Near and Middle East, Darlington continues, that the effects of mutation, hybridization, and natural selection produced the highest breeds of men. The hunting and gathering peoples on the periphery of these land masses were subject to less hybridization and genetic recombination and hence remained less inventive and gifted than their more fortunately situated brethren.

> The paleolithic hunter, like the gipsy in Europe, is a wanderer. He has always lived by wandering and all his instincts are adjusted to the needs of wandering, adjusted to resist settlement. Nothing but hybridization will change him. His instincts reappear in some classes, professions, and peoples of advanced societies and are altogether excluded from others. His fecklessness, his interest in killing game, his yearning for movement are found at the top and at the bottom of society. . . .[33]

Shades of Thorstein Veblen and his *Theory of the Leisure Class!* It was the "new men" of Europe and Asia, Darlington argues, who spread gradually over the whole earth because of their ability to invent new kinds of tools and use them in new ways. These inventions, in turn, promoted the survival and multiplication of the "new men." The result was "a step forward in the long selective process of the mental improvement of mankind." With mental improvement came art, magic, religion, and myth, all expressing man's joy and terror at the discovery of his new powers. In the third millenium B.C., various processes of hybridization produced the Hebrew and the Phoenician peoples and the hybrid priesthood of the Jews. The highly gifted Jewish priests devoted their intellectual powers to "the most successful study of social behaviour and of its biological causes and consequences" ever undertaken and promulgated as a result of a code of social ethics with religious sanctions admirably adapted to ensure the survival and multiplication of the Jewish people.

> Religion they held to be the prime means of this survival since religion was the business of binding people together. And they came to regard the history of the people and of the religion as the chief instrument to be used in this grand design.[34]

Besides these social-scientist priests, says Darlington, there were the Hebrew prophets, "men who by their individual genetic character utterly rejected the environment they lived in and by doing so created a new environment." Their prophetic utterances, dramatizing the polarity "between the transient interest of the political state and the durable interests of individual belief and integrity," embodied sound practical policy as well as profound spiritual doctrine. The prophetic idea of the "saving remnant" reflected the prophets' recognition that the achievements of the Jews were the outcome of genetic differences among the tribes of Israel, "differences connected with their habit of life."

> Each of the later conflicts [among tribes] was followed by the selection and differential multiplication of one line or stock or tribe at the expense of the other. In the language of the prophets this was a process of *winnowing*, a process they and their people very well understood. . . .
>
> It was Isaiah first, and then Ezekiel, who gave precision to this doctrine of the "survival of the remnants." It is a doctrine which has been rightly compared with the biological principle of the "survival of the fittest."[35]

Thus, Jewish religious literature, "one of the high points of human achievement," was the outcome of underlying genetic changes.

> It covered in its range every aspect of great literature and of human achievement save one: that of humour, or wit or fun. That is a side of human nature and literature that appeared in the contemporaries of Job in Greece. It came from Europe and Africa. And it appeared among the later Jews after they had incorporated other racial elements from Europe and Africa; that is after another racial assimilation.[35]

Here with a vengeance is the Spencerian-Darwinian doctrine that the progress of mankind is brought about by a gradual improvement in the instinctual and intellectual endowment of the surviving human race, a doctrine now pruned of the inherited effects of mental and moral training and based solely on natural selection and hybridization. The elder Huxley's moral intuitionism is here grounded in the genetic constitution of the Hebrew prophets. The noble ideals and spiritual insights of the Bible, favoring "moral and intellectual integrity at the expense of superstition," are presented as the incidental result of a priestly strategy designed to secure the survival and multiplication of the Jews. "And it succeeded. It proved to be true. For in fact Babylon fell and the Jews survived."[37]

The rest of Darlington's book is of a piece with what has been described. The genetic approach to history, declares Darlington, has made possible a unified history of man. And it was Darwin who pointed the way to this unified history.

> He showed man as an animal, an organism that could and must be studied as an animal, using all the scientific methods that can be applied to any other animal. This meant that, in his physical, emotional and mental properties, his individual, social and racial character, in his diseases and in his speech, in his behaviour and in his beliefs, he was a proper object of experimental study; and in all these respects his evolution was subject to the principles of natural selection with all its special forms of sexual selection, artificial selection and unconscious selection.[38]

Francis Galton, says Darlington, followed in Darwin's footsteps by studying human intelligence scientifically and applying this new knowledge to problems of history and to the sociology of primitive and advanced societies. Alexander Carr-Saunders showed that human societies, like animal societies, regulate their reproduction by instinctive moral controls. The historian N. D. Fustel de Coulanges recognized that social stratification in cities was based on racial differences. W. H. Rivers, Lord Raglan, and Lewis Henry Morgan studied the effects of inbreeding and outbreeding and the social customs designed to promote or retard these. Walter Bagehot and others developed the notion of a social environment determined by the genetic character of the individuals comprising a society. Archaeology, with the aid of radiocarbon dating, established the directions of movement of peoples, and genetics showed how to interpret the historical record as the necessary outcome of changes in social systems regulating inbreeding and outbreeding. Outbreeding, says Darlington, produces creative individuals, "men of destiny" who powerfully affect their times, but it also produces the social misfit, the delinquent or criminal.

> He [the misfit] is the price that has to be paid for hybridization. He is the burden that has to be carried by society as a whole in return for the most adaptable breeding system. Fortunately he is, as a rule, of reduced viability and fertility. Natural selection has in this way so far prevented the burden from becoming intolerable.[39]

What, then, is the duty and destiny of man in the light of these revelations of genetics and other sciences? His ultimate destiny, says Darlington, is "probably extinction." In the meantime his duty is to strive to maintain maximum genetic diversity.

> Man's future prospects are proportionate to the amount of genetic diversity he maintains among the interfertile members of his own species. In this respect, more than in any other, the loss of any primitive and apparently unsuccessful tribe affects the future of mankind as a whole. In this respect mankind is one; and for us men are undoubtedly the most precious of animals.

> In order to preserve him [the primitive tribesman] it is not enough that we refrain from killing him. We have also to preserve the diverse habitats which diverse peoples need for their survival . . . from damage which civilization has so far so wantonly wrought upon them.[40]

Here, at last, is the reductio ad absurdum of the biological interpretation of history. After all the fine talk about the "achievements" of man, about the various "improvements" that have marked his "progress" on earth, about the "creative elements of his social, intellectual or spiritual life," about the "moral and intellectual integrity" of the individual, we discover that it is all a matter of genes, of inbreeding and outbreeding (hopefully regulated wisely by clever priests who know how to use religion for genetic purposes), and that uncivilized peoples are to be preserved and protected, not because they have any inherent dignity or sanctity or natural rights as human beings, but because their destruction might hasten the extinction of homo sapiens, the "most precious" of animals in his own estimation.

> To be sure [writes Darlington], the restricted specialized habitats of civilization give the greatest opportunities for what we . . . are pleased to call intelligence. But we have now learnt that intelligence is of many kinds. It has to be measured not on one scale but on many. And its diversity, if lost, cannot easily be recovered.[41]

That human intelligence uncontrolled by reason or religion may be the gravest threat of all to human survival seems not to have occurred to Darlington.

One might suppose that the Darwinian interpretation of human nature, society, and history had been carried as far as it could go in Darlington's treatise, but the "speculative essay" *On Human Nature* (1978) by the Harvard sociobiologist Edward O. Wilson proves the contrary. Like George Gaylord Simpson, Wilson portrays evolution as a "mechanistic process" devoid of immanent purpose or final goal. The human brain, he declares, is an unforeseen product of this mechanistic process. It exists "because it promotes the survival and multiplication of the genes that direct its assembly." The mind, in turn, is "an epiphenomenon of the neuronal machinery of the brain," "a device for survival and reproduction," and reason is "just one of its various techniques."[42] A mechanistic process capable of constructing "devices," an epiphenomenon with reason as one of its "techniques"!

According to Wilson, this epiphenomenon, the human mind, is capable not only of understanding the mechanistic process that produced it but also of discovering the laws of historical development that Vico, Marx, Spencer, Spengler, and Toynbee searched for in vain because they lacked a scientific understanding of human nature. Once this understanding has been provided by sociobiology, says Wilson, it will become apparent that "the culture of each society travels along one or the other set of evolutionary trajectories whose full array is constrained by the genetic rules of human nature." "As the social sciences mature into predictive disciplines," he adds, "the permissible trajectories will not only diminish in number but our descendants will be able to sight farther along them."[43] Finally, as man's knowledge of the genetic basis of his own nature grows, he will be in a position to choose a system of values on an objective basis and chart the future development of the human species, eugenically and otherwise.

The "objective basis" for these harrowing decisions will be provided by biological science. This science, says Wilson, tells us that the entire gene pool of the human species must be preserved at maximum diversity. It would be dangerous to the prospects for evolutionary progress to allow any tribe, however primitive, to become extinct. Biology also dictates respect for universal human rights, "because we are mammals."

> Our societies are based on the mammalian plan; the individual strives for personal reproductive success foremost and that of his immediate kin secondarily; further grudging cooperation represents a compromise struck in order to enjoy the benefits of group membership. . . . We will accede to universal rights because power is too fluid in advanced technological societies to circumvent this mammalian imperative; the long-term consequences of inequity will always be visibly dangerous to its temporary benefi-

ciaries. I suggest that this is the true reason for the universal rights movement and that an understanding of its raw biological causation will be more compelling in the end than any rationalization contrived by culture to reinforce and euphemize it.[44]

So much for Jefferson's God-given unalienable rights of man and Kant's categorical imperative! The mammalian imperative supersedes them.

But Wilson, like Auguste Comte before him, recognizes that the "mythopoeic drive" is deeply rooted in human nature and that no amount of scientific analysis will prevent men and women from elaborating religious systems and mythologies and endowing them with moral energy. "When blind ideologies and religious beliefs are stripped away, others are quickly manufactured as replacements." The problem, therefore, is to harness the mythopoeic drive in the service of "the rational search for human progress." This can only be done—here again Wilson concurs with Comte—by substituting the mythology of scientific materialism for the mythologies that have inspired mankind to the present time. Scientific materialism *is* a mythology ("in the noble sense"), Wilson concedes, but its superior quality as myth is attested by many things: "its repeated triumphs in explaining and controlling the physical world; its self-correcting nature open to all competent to devise and conduct the tests; its readiness to examine all subjects sacred and profane; and now the possibility of explaining traditional religion by the mechanistic models of evolutionary biology." This last achievement, says Wilson, will be crucial.

> If religion, including the dogmatic secular ideologies [such as Marxism], can be systematically analyzed and explained as a product of the brain's evolution, its power as an external source of morality will be gone forever and the solution of the second dilemma [that of finding a substitute mythology] will have become a practical necessity.[45]

The core of the substitute mythology, says Wilson, is "the evolutionary epic."

> Let me repeat its minimum claims: that the laws of the physical sciences are consistent with those of the biological and social

sciences and can be linked in chains of causal explanation; that life and mind have a physical basis; that the world as we know it has evolved from earlier worlds obedient to the same laws; and that the visible universe today is everywhere subject to these materialist explanations. The epic can be indefinitely strengthened up and down the line, but its most sweeping assertions cannot be proved with finality.[48]

But this epic, like all epics, needs a hero. The hero, it turns out, is "mind," the same human mind that Wilson has already told us will ultimately be explained (presumably by itself) as "an epiphenomenon of the neuronal machinery of the brain," which, in turn, is an accidental product of natural selection.

Paradox can go no further. The familiar paradoxes of Christianity—man's God-created but fallen nature, human freedom and divine foreknowledge, the mystery of the Trinity—are as nothing compared to the mysteries and paradoxes of Wilson's evolutionary epic: its ordered universe without an Orderer, its progress from blind force to conscious intellect and will without any immanent purpose or direction, its heroic epiphenomenal human mind produced by evolutionary chance but capable of comprehending the forces that produced it and using them for good or ill, its morally responsible beings in an amoral universe, its faith in the power of science to provide ethical and spiritual as well as practical guidance for mankind, its naive confidence in the ultimate beneficence of sheer intellect, its fearful ignorance of human perversity, its insensitivity to the tragic dimension of human life. Do these Darwinistic treatises, old and new, convey to the mind a picture of man as an unbound Prometheus plumbing the secrets of nature and human nature in his "rational search for human progress," as Wilson suggests? Or do they rather bring to mind a hero of Greek tragedy driven relentlessly on by hubris, by overweening pride, rising sunward on Icarian wings? Even more aptly, do they suggest the Biblical portrait of man as a God-like creature endowed with high potentialities but forever falling short of them, stubbornly striving through his powers of intellect to throw off his creatureliness and make himself master of his own destiny, and thereby becoming the agent of his own destruction?

To the historian of ideas it seems evident that these champions of evolutionary biology as the clue to human duty and destiny are caught on the scientistic horn of the positivist dilemma. Whoever regards science as man's sole means of acquiring reliable knowledge of reality must eventually confront that dilemma. If science and the scientific method are defined narrowly so as to exclude value judgments and all non-logico-experimental statements (to use Vilfredo Pareto's term), it then becomes impossible to say why anything, science included, is important or valuable, why the passion for truth is to be inculcated and respected, or why human beings have any more inherent dignity than starfish or stones. But if, on the contrary, science is declared competent to discover human duty and destiny, as those who choose the other horn of the dilemma assert, one is soon confronted with the conflicting claims of Huxleyan science, Darlingtonian science, Freudian science, Marxian science, Comtean science, and a host of other scientisms. In the ensuing struggle the central idea of science as an enterprise in which all qualified observers can agree as to what the evidence proves vanishes from sight. Thus, whichever horn of the dilemma the positivist takes, science is the loser.

In any case, it seems clear that with respect to the fundamental problems of philosophy the post-Darwinian writers are, as T. H. Huxley said long ago, "exactly where the pre-Darwinian generations were." What is nature? What is mind? How are they related? What is man? If man is part and parcel of nature, must not nature in some sense be like man? But if man can comprehend nature and set himself against it or direct its course, must he not transcend nature? And how can nature be comprehensible to man's mind if that mind is totally unlike it? These are old questions, as old as philosophy itself, and from what we have seen of Darwinism as a world view it seems unlikely that evolutionary biology in and of itself will ever provide intelligible answers to them. Shall we not, then, resume the age-old quest for knowledge of reality in a humbler spirit, acknowledging our debt to science for all it can tell us about ourselves and nature but realizing that the ultimate intelligibility of things, if there is one, is *not* scientific in the sense that we understand that word today. If human life were to come to an end fifty or one hundred years from now through human pollution of the natural environment, the event would presumably have a scientific explanation. But would the explanation satisfy anyone—even Sir Julian Huxley?

NOTES

1. See earlier, p.85.

2. T. H. Huxley, "The Genealogy of Animals," in *Darwiniana: Essays* (New York: D. Appleton and Co., 1908), p. 113. Originally published in 1869.

3. T. H. Huxley, *Evolution and Ethics and Other Essays* (London: Macmillan, 1895), pp. 82–83. In a brief reply to a review of Huxley's Romanes Lecture in the *Athenaeum* for July 22, 1893, Herbert Spencer denied that he had based ethics on the struggle for existence and quoted one of Huxley's own footnotes to his Romanes Lecture to the effect that " 'strictly speaking, social life and the ethical process, in virtue of which it advances towards perfection, are part and parcel of the general process of evolution, just as the gregarious habit of innumerable plants and animals, which has been of immense advantage to them, is so.' " Spencer then remarks: "If the ethical process is a part of the process of evolution or cosmic process, then how can the two be put in opposition?" See Spencer, *Various Fragments* (New York: D. Appleton and Co., 1898), p. 122.

4. T. H. Huxley to N. P. Clayton, Hodeslea, Eastbourne, 4 November 1892, quoted in Leonard Huxley, ed., *Life and Letters of Thomas Henry Huxley* (London: Macmillan, 1900), 3: 223–224. In the same letter Huxley finds a partial basis for social ethics in reflection on human experience: "The end of society is peace and mutual protection, so that the individual may reach the fullest and highest life attainable by man. The rules of conduct by which this end is to be attained are discoverable—like the other so-called laws of Nature— by observation and experiment and only in that way." Then follows his discussion of the "moral sense." See also his *Science and Hebrew Tradition: Essays* (London: Macmillan, 1893), pp. 161–162, where he quotes Micah's injunction to love mercy, and so forth, as an example of the Hebrew prophets' "wonderful . . . inspiration of genius," adding: "But what extent of knowledge, what acuteness of scientific criticism, can touch this? . . . Will the progress of research prove that

justice is worthless and mercy hateful; will it ever soften the bitter contrast between our actions and our aspirations; or show us the bounds of the universe, and bid us say, Go to, now we comprehend the infinite?" Huxley was a humanist at heart, but his heart and his head were often at war with each other, and whoever tries to reconcile his conflicting statements will experience great difficulty. Huxley was doubtless right that "science takes for its province only that which is susceptible of clear intellectual comprehension," but his positivistic credo made him restrict the subjects susceptible of clear intellectual comprehension to those dealt with by science, consigning all other forms of inquiry to the realm of imagination, hope, and ignorance. See *Science and Hebrew Tradition*, pp. 160–161.

5. T. H. Huxley, "Evolution and Ethics. Prolegomena," in *Evolution and Ethics*, p. 37. First published in 1894.

6. Ibid., p. 36.

7. Ibid., pp. 44–45.

8. Julian Huxley, *Evolution in Action* (New York: New American Library, 1953), p. 31.

9. George Gaylord Simpson, *This View of Life: The World of an Evolutionist* (New York: Harcourt, Brace and World, Inc., 1964), pp. 27–28, 37. Concerning the essays in this book Simpson says in his preface: "All the previously published essays have been revised, some slightly and some radically, to bring them up to date, to eliminate repetition, and to coordinate them into a unity. . . ."

10. Julian Huxley, *Evolution: The Modern Synthesis* (New York and London: Harper & Bros., 1943), pp. 562 and 566. See also Huxley, *Evolution in Action*, chaps. 3 and 5.

11. For an extended discussion of the ambiguous role of the idea of progress in modern evolutionary biology see my essay "Evolution and Progress," *Johns Hopkins Magazine* 14 (1962): 8 ff.

12. Julian Huxley, *Evolution in Action*, p. 10. How far Huxley has departed from the nineteenth-century law-bound system of matter in motion may be seen on page 77:

> For a biologist, much the easiest way is to think of mind and matter as two aspects of a single, underlying reality—shall we call it world substance, the stuff out of which the world is made. . . . In this view, mental activities are among the inevitable properties of world substance when this is organized in the form of the particular kind of biological machinery we find in a brain. . . . I find myself driven to assume . . . that all living substance has mental, or we had better say mindlike, properties; but that these are, for the most part, far below the level of detection. They could

only be utilized for biological ends when organs were evolved capable of intensifying them.

13. Julian Huxley, "Introduction" to the second edition of *Evolution: The Modern Synthesis* (1963), quoted in Philip Appleman, ed., *Darwin* (New York: W. W. Norton, 1970), p. 342.

14. Julian Huxley, *Evolution in Action*, pp. 125–126.

15. Ibid., p. 119.

16. Ibid., p. 135.

17. George Gaylord Simpson, *The Meaning of Evolution: A Study of the History of Life and of Its Significance for Man* (New Haven: Yale University Press, 1949), p. 278. This work preceded Huxley's *Evolution in Action* but drew on his *Evolution: The Modern Synthesis*.

18. Simpson, *The Meaning of Evolution*, pp. 245–246.

19. Ibid., pp. 261–262.

20. Ibid., pp. 343–344. See also p. 284.

21. Ibid., p. 241.

22. Ibid., pp. 310–311.

23. Ibid., p. 311.

24. Ibid., pp. 310, 313. Simpson notes in a footnote on page 283 that his ethical conclusions are similar to those of Julian Huxley and attributes their agreement to the fact that both have "a common basis in the modern synthetic theory of evolution."

25. Ibid., p. 281.

26. Ibid., pp. 336–337.

27. Ibid., p. 332.

28. George Gaylord Simpson, *This View of Life*, pp. 80–81.

29. Ibid., p. 105.

30. Ibid., p. 107.

31. In Darwin's reprint collection at the Cambridge University Library is a pamphlet entitled *Political Liberty and the Best Means for Its Attainment by the Natives of India*, sent to Darwin by the author, "A Young Hindu." The pamphlet stresses the operation of the law of natural selection in human history. On the title page Darwin wrote: "A Hindoo who perceives that natural selection will apply to nations!" See also the essay "Darwin as a Social Evolutionist" in the present volume.

32. Cyril D. Darlington, *The Evolution of Man and Society* (New York: Simon and Schuster, 1971), p. 25.

33. Ibid., p. 30.

34. Ibid., p. 178.

35. Ibid., p. 190.

36. Ibid., p. 192.

37. Ibid., p. 190.

38. Ibid., p. 671.

39. Ibid., p. 678.

40. Ibid., p. 679.

41. Ibid.

42. Edward O. Wilson, *On Human Nature* (Cambridge, Mass.: Harvard University Press, 1978), p. 2.

43. Ibid., p. 208.

44. Ibid., p. 199.

45. Ibid., p. 201.

46. Ibid.

SUGGESTED FURTHER READING

On the subject of naturalistic ethics, see Anthony G. N. Flew, *Evolutionary Ethics* (London: Macmillan, 1967); George E. Pugh, *The Biological Origin of Human Values* (New York: Basic Books, 1977); Raymond B. Cattell, *A New Morality from Science: Beyondism* (New York: Pergamon Press, 1972); W. F. Quillian, Jr. *The Moral Theory of Evolutionary Naturalism* (New Haven: Yale University Press, 1945); C. H. Waddington, *The Ethical Animal* (New York: Atheneum, 1961); W. Hudson, ed., *New Studies in Ethics* (London: Macmillan, 1967). See also the footnotes to part 3, "Evolution, Humanity, and Ethics," of Simpson's *The Meaning of Evolution* and Julian Huxley's "Evolutionary Ethics" and the "Notes" appended to it in T. H. Huxley and Julian Huxley, *Touchstone for Ethics, 1893–1943* (New York and London: Harper & Bros., 1947), pp. 113–166.

For a historical view of the role played by the concept of progress in evolutionary biology, see George Gaylord Simpson, "The Concept of Progress in Organic Evolution," *Social Research* 41 (1974): 28–51; Henryk Skolimowski, "The Scientific World View and the Illusions of Progress," ibid., pp. 52–82; L. Sh. Davitashvili, *The Problem of Evolutionary Progress (The Theory of Aromorphosis)* (in Russian with brief summaries in English) (Tbilisi: Metsniereba, 1972); John C.

Greene, "Evolution and Progress," *The Johns Hopkins Magazine* 14 (1962): 8–12, 32.

For an excellent selection of critiques of Wilson's *Sociobiology* from various points of view—scientific, ethical, political—see Arthur L. Caplan, ed., *The Sociobiology Debate: Readings on Ethical and Scientific Issues* (New York: Harper & Row, 1978). For a critique of the positivistic world view of some evolutionary biologists see Leszek Kolakowski, *The Alienation of Reason: A History of Positivist Thought*, Norbert Guterman, trans. (Garden City, N. Y.: Doubleday, 1968) and Richard Spilsbury, *Providence Lost: A Critique of Darwinism* (London: Oxford University Press, 1974). See also Derek Freeman, "Sociobiology: The 'Anti-discipline' of Anthropology," in Ashley Montagu, ed., *Sociobiology Examined* (New York: Oxford University Press, 1980) and "Towards an Anthropology Both Scientific and Humanistic," *Canberra Anthropology* I (1978), pp. 44–68.

POSTSCRIPT

In the last two essays I have attempted to delineate a world view that emerged about the same time as the Darwin-Wallace theory of evolution by natural selection, incorporating it as an essential feature, and to trace the subsequent modifications of that world view in the writings of some twentieth-century Darwinians. In short, I have tried to define a species of the genus "evolutionary naturalism" and to study its evolution. I realize, however, that the account I have given of its career in the twentieth century is very incomplete. Julian Huxley, George Gaylord Simpson, Cyril Darlington, and Edward O. Wilson are good examples of the Darwinian species, but they are only a few representatives of a numerous breed. To give a full description of the species with all its varieties would require a lengthy volume, especially if one were to attempt not simply to display the influence of their scientific researches on their world view but also to analyze the influence of their positivistic, naturalistic world view on their science. In fairness, one should also take account of the views of evolutionary biologists like Theodosius Dobzhansky, L. C. Birch, Teilhard de Chardin, and others whose world view is not only theistic but specifically Christian. These are tasks I hope to undertake in the near future.

One should also reckon with those biologists who view evolution in thermodynamical terms, relegating natural selection to a subsidiary role in the overall process. For these biologists Herbert Spencer plays the prophetic role the Darwinians assign to Darwin. Thus, Peter Rich, an ecologist at the University of Connecticut, writes:

> I agree with your emphasis on Spencer's philosophical contribution to Darwinism, but I would suggest that convergence upon a point

of view is not the same as convergence upon a point. If one starts with Spencer's integrated philosophy, from which the assumptions of a law-bound universe and a principle of "progress" emerge, and places Darwin's scientific exposition of natural selection at the proper (lesser) level of abstraction and in the appropriate biological quadrant of Spencer's universe, one creates an axis which, when viewed end on, provides a point of view upon which all might be said to converge. This convergence is a useful observation for an historian interested in the chronological acquisition of knowledge, but a red herring for scientists, for whom position along the Spencer-Darwin axis is more critical than convergence upon the axis.

Given this construction of the "Darwinian convergence," I have no complaint about the term "Darwinism." However, I am becoming convinced that the scientists who operate at the Darwinian (scientific) end of the axis without reference to the philosophical (Spencerian) end are doing science in a "business as usual," ultimately non-progressive mode without responding to critically important problems threatening civilization. . . .

Spencer was co-opted by the more objective and scientific but less philosophically integrated demonstration of evolution in eukaryotes by Darwin and Wallace, which had little recourse to fundamental causes. For Spencer, Darwin's elegant exposition of secondary causes (heritable variation, struggle for existence, and natural selection) was but a special case of the evolutionary process. Spencer readily accepted natural selection, along with the now discredited idea of inheritance of acquired characters, as further evidence of his unified philosophy, but his philosophy transcended both. . . . Darwin explained how evolution works, not why it works.[1]

Rich concludes that entropy was the cause, rather than the result, of life in the pre-Cambrian period and that natural selection was the result, rather than the cause, of evolution broadly conceived.

In view of my negative evaluation of the philosophical conclusions reached by Huxley, Simpson, Darlington, and Wilson, the reader may wish to know my own position with respect to the issues raised by these writers. In this connection I cannot do better than to quote from a letter I wrote in response to a request that I declare whether I was a "cosmic teleologist" and, if so, explain my conception as to "the force or agent or person who directs the cosmic teleology." To this request I replied:

> I have no systematically elaborated cosmology or metaphysics. It seems obvious to me, however, that if one attempts to conceive reality as an evolutionary process that has produced and is producing higher and higher levels of order and value, one must presuppose some creative ground of the process capable of envisaging its possibilities. Otherwise the conception makes no sense, and we wind up in Julian Huxley's absurdities.
>
> On the ethical question, I think that history shows that profound ethical systems can be and have been elaborated by philosophical reflection on human experience without reference to evolutionary biology. Ultimately, of course, one's ideas about the conduct of life are grounded in one's view of reality and man's place therein. If ultimate reality is really as Simpson, Huxley, and Wilson represent it, the rational man will be more likely to take Hobbes's ethical advice and seek peace at all costs than to pretend with Huxley et al. that biology ratifies the Biblical injunction to do justly and love mercy or the Enlightenment doctrine of universal human rights. But if, on the contrary, God exists and if He has revealed himself to us in his Son, then we know beyond a shadow of a doubt that we ought also to love one another.

The historian of ideas cannot be expected to be a profound metaphysician and moral philosopher, but his search for the presuppositions underlying the thought of an age and the factors responsible for changes in those presuppositions must eventually bring him face to face with the deepest questions human beings can ask. It must also make him realize what a profound influence the answers men and women give to these questions can have on human history. If I have been strongly critical of the claims made for evolutionary science as the best and safest guide to human duty and destiny, it is as much out of concern for the integrity and autonomy of science as for the interests of philosophy and religion. As I have said elsewhere:

> Every great scientific synthesis stimulates efforts to view the whole of reality in its terms, and Darwin's theory of natural selection was no exception. But the views of reality that originate in this way are not themselves scientific, nor are they subject to

scientific verification. They attempt to make sense not only of the facts "out there," held at arm's length by the observer, but also of the facts "in here," facts such as our awareness of our own act of existence, our appreciation of beauty, our sense of moral account-ability, our communion with source of being. Facts of the latter kind lie close to the heart of reality, but they do not lend themselves to scientific formulation. Attempts to explain them scientifically end by explaining them away. But science itself then becomes unintelligible.[2]

To ignore the differences between science, philosophy, and religion and roll them all into one evolutionary gospel claiming to disclose the meaning of existence is as dangerous to science as it is to philosophy and religion. If scientists aspire to be prophets and preachers, they cannot expect society to grant them the relative autonomy they have enjoyed in Western culture in recent centuries. The current misguided campaign to require the teaching of "creationist biology" alongside evolutionary biology is sufficient evidence of that. The hard-won ideal of disinterested inquiry guided by insight and logic but rigorously controlled by generally accepted methods of empirical testing is too precious an acquisition of the human spirit to be sacrificed to grandiose but delusory and self-destructive dreams of an omnicompetent science of nature-history, society, and human duty and destiny. As a student of the history of ideas, I am convinced that science, ideology, and world view will forever be intertwined and interacting. As a citizen concerned for the welfare of science and of mankind generally, however, I cannot but hope that scientists will recognize where science ends and other things begin.

NOTES

1. Personal communication from Professor Peter Rich, Depart-ment of Biology, University of Connecticut.

2. John C. Greene, *Darwin and the Modern World View* (Baton Rouge: Louisiana State University Press, 1961), pp. 132–133.

INDEX